ROCKHURST COLLEGE LIBRARY

0 0006 00756191

Date Due

D0965776

ANALYSIS OF COVARIANCE

Albert R. Wildt
Olli T. Ahtola

Series: Quantitative Applications
in the Social Sciences

a SAGE **UNIVERSITY** PAPER

12

SAGE **UNIVERSITY** PAPERS

Series: Quantitative Applications in the Social Sciences

Series Editor: **Michael S. Lewis-Beck,** *University of Iowa*

Editorial Consultants

Frank Andrews, *Institute of Social Research, University of Michigan*
Richard A. Berk, *Sociology, University of California, Los Angeles*
H. Russell Bernard, *Anthropology, University of Florida, Gainesville*
William Berry, *Political Science, University of Kentucky*
Kenneth A. Bollen, *Sociology, University of North Carolina, Chapel Hill*
H. D. Hoover, *College of Education, University of Iowa*
Richard M. Jaeger, *Education, University of North Carolina, Greensboro*
Roger E. Kirk, *Psychology, Baylor University*
Peter Marsden, *Social Relations, Harvard University*
Terence McDonald, *History, University of Michigan*
Helmut Norpoth, *Political Science, SUNY at Stony Brook*
Douglas Rivers, *Political Science, University of California, Los Angeles*
Gilbert Sax, *Education and Psychology, University of Washington*
Herbert Weisberg, *Political Science, Ohio State University*

Publisher

Sara Miller McCune, Sage Publications, Inc.

Series / Number 07-012

ANALYSIS OF COVARIANCE

ALBERT R. WILDT
University of Georgia and
University of Florida

OLLI AHTOLA
University of Florida

SAGE PUBLICATIONS
The Publishers of Professional Social Science
Newbury Park   London   New Delhi

Copyright © 1978 by Sage Publications, Inc.

Printed in the United States of America

All rights reserved. No part of this book may be reproduced
or utilized in any form or by any means, electronic or mechanical,
including photocopying, recording, or by any
information storage and retrieval system, without permission in writing
from the publisher.

For information address:

SAGE Publications, Inc.
2111 West Hillcrest Drive
Newbury Park, California 91320

SAGE Publications Ltd.
28 Banner Street
London EC1Y 8QE
England

SAGE Publications India Pvt. Ltd.
M-32 Market
Greater Kailash I
New Delhi 110 048 India

International Standard Book Number 0-8039-1164-5

Library of Congress Catalog Card No. L.C. 78-64330

ELEVENTH PRINTING, 1990

When citing a professional paper, please use the proper form. Remember to cite the
correct Sage University Paper series title and include the paper number. One of the
two following formats can be adapted (depending on the style manual used):

(1) IVERSEN, GUDMUND R. and NORPOTH, HELMUT (1976) "Analysis of
Variance." Sage University Paper series on Quantitative Applications in the Social
Sciences, 07-001. Beverly Hills and London: Sage Pubns.

OR

(2) Iversen, Gudmund R. and Norpoth, Helmut. 1976. *Analysis of Variance*. Sage
University Paper series on Quantitative Applications in the Social Sciences, series no.
07-001. Beverly Hills and London: Sage Publications.

HA
33
W 46

ROCKHURST COLLEGE LIBRARY

CONTENTS

132238

Editor's Introduction

ANALYSIS OF COVARIANCE by Albert Wildt and Olli Ahtola builds nicely on the earlier fine paper in this series, ANALYSIS OF VARIANCE, by Gudmund Iversen and Helmut Norpoth. The reader should either be familiar with analysis of variance, or should study the Iversen and Norpoth volume carefully before undertaking this paper. Another helpful prerequisite is knowledge of regression analysis, at least at the introductory level.

Analysis of covariance is useful in both experimental and nonexperimental research. It is a statistical technique based upon the general linear model, and as such can be presented as an extension of either analysis of variance or of regression analysis, or of both. Wildt and Ahtola emphasize the relationship with analysis of variance and with experimental designs, but do not ignore its use in nonexperimental work and its relationship with regression.

Basically, analysis of covariance is useful when the researcher wishes to examine the relationships among at least two quantitative variables and at least one additional categorical (qualitative) variable. (Provided, of course, that certain assumptions are met and the technique is therefore appropriate. Wildt and Ahtola delineate these assumptions at length.) One may be interested in examining the relationship between two quantitative variables but find that a categorical variable is confounding that relationship. Analysis of covariance then allows one to examine the relationship in question "controlling for" this confounding categorical variable.

Another use of analysis of covariance would be to examine the relationship between a quantitative dependent variable and a categorical independent variable, with a second quantitative variable as the nuisance factor. We can examine the differences on the dependent variable among categories of the independent variable "controlling for" differences on the nuisance quantitative variable. Wildt and Ahtola provide numerous examples of the use of analysis of covariance, and note that it is generally used to:

- Increase the precision of randomized experiments, by providing a statistical control for extraneous variables, when direct control through the design of the experiment is impractical or impossible.

[5]

- Statistically remove pre-existing differences among groups which are used in experimental tests but which must be assigned intact to various treatment conditions.

- Remove differences on the dependent variable, in observational studies, among naturally occurring groups which are due to differences in extraneous variables.

- Perform a type of regression analysis which controls for categorical variables when examining the relationship between two or more quantitative variables.

Wildt and Ahtola provide examples of the appropriate uses of analysis of covariance from a number of disciplines, including sociology, political science, behavioral research in architectural design, education, and a continuing example of a hypothetical experiment on the impact of introducing liquor in rural municipalities in Finland.

In the latter example, a long-standing Finnish law which allowed the sale of liquor *only* in urban areas was repealed. An experiment was performed in which rural municipalities were assigned to three groups: one group where each municipality received a package store, another group each of which received both a package store and a licensed restaurant, and a third group which received neither. The study was designed to examine the impact of the introduction of liquor on traffic accidents, and since the prior rate is a confounding variable, it was traffic accidents, and since the prior rate is a confounding variable, it was decided to use it as a "covariate" in an analysis of covariance (see text for why they did not simply use a change score as their dependent variable). In effect, the question was whether or not the two treatment levels had an impact on traffic accident rates, controlling for prior accident rates, and if so, what type of impact. Read on, and learn not only the procedures and uses of analysis of covariance but whether booze kills more than one way.

—John L. Sullivan, Editoral Board

1. INTRODUCTION

Overview of Analysis of Covariance

Numerous situations arise in the social sciences where interest centers on the relationship or association between two variables or among a number of variables. For example, a political scientist may wish to contrast voting frequency by sex and/or income, or a sociologist may be concerned with the relationship between mobility and the age of the head of the household. In cases where such measurement of association is of concern, the statistical procedure employed by the researcher is, in part, determined by the nature of the variables under consideration.

Considering only instances involving a single dependent variable, a number of different cases may be constructed according to whether the independent and dependent variables are quantitative or qualitative in nature. Quantitative variables are interval- or ratio-scaled (e.g., age expressed in years or income expressed in dollars), and qualitative variables are categorical and include both nominal- and ordinal-scaled measures (e.g., sex or religion). Those cases in which the dependent variable is qualitative or categorical are not of primary concern to the following discussion and are not considered.

Instances involving a single quantitative dependent variable may be classified into one of three cases. Case 1 involves one or more qualitative (categorical) independent variables. In this context the researcher is usually investigating the possibility of differences in the average value of the dependent variable over the various categories of the independent variable(s). An analysis procedure appropriate for case 1 is analysis of variance. (The reader is referred to Iverson and Norpoth [1976] for a discussion of analysis of variance.) Case 2 involves quantitative independent variables. In this context the researcher is usually investigating for possible changes in the dependent variable which may accompany changes in the independent variable(s). Correlation and regression analysis are appropriate procedures here. Case 3 involves both quantitative and qualitative independent variables. This case is of primary concern for the present discussion, and two alternate (though statistically similar) procedures are available for analyzing situations which meet this condition. They are analysis of covariance and regression analysis with dummy variables. It is analysis of covariance which is of concern in the discussion to follow.

Analysis of covariance is a special case of the linear model, just as are the regression and the analysis of variance models. Traditionally, regression analysis has been used in conjunction with survey designs or observational data, and analysis of variance with experimental designs. Analysis of covariance, which is a combination of the two techniques, can be discussed as either an extension of regression analysis or as an extension of analysis of variance. This is quite natural because the technique is useful whether the underlying design is experimental, quasi-experimental or purely observational—without any experimental control or manipulation.

Because of the relationship of analysis of covariance to regression analysis and analysis of variance, an understanding of the basic concepts of these two procedures is essential to the understanding of analysis of covariance. Accordingly, in the discussion presented in this paper it is assumed that the reader possesses this necessary basic knowledge of analysis of variance and regression analysis.

Alternate Problem Perspectives with Analysis of Covariance

Within the class of problems involving a quantitative dependent variable and both quantitative and qualitative independent variables, there are three different problem perspectives which are commonly encountered. Analysis of covariance may be used with each of these perspectives. The first perspective, which we designate as the experimental perspective, involves those instances when interest centers on the differences occurring in the dependent variable over the categories, or levels of the qualitative independent variable(s). In these cases it is assumed that one or more quantitative independent variables, referred to as covariates, influence the dependent variable in a linear fashion, and independently of the level or category of the qualitative independent variable(s); but this relationship is *not of primary concern* to the researcher (the covariate is considered a nuisance variable). The quantitative independent variable (covariate) is included in the analysis either to remove extraneous variation from the dependent variable, and thereby, increase the precision of the analysis, or to remove bias due to the groups not being matched on that quantitative independent variable. The analysis procedure in this case can be viewed as adjusting the dependent variable for differences in the covariate and then investigating the relationship between the qualitative independent variable(s) and the adjusted values of the dependent variable. This type of situation arises in the case of both observational studies and designed experiments. It is this case which is covered in considerable detail in succeeding sections.

The second problem perspective is exemplified by those situations in which primary concern centers upon the relationship between the dependent variable and the quantitative independent variable(s) or covariate(s). In these cases one or more categorical, or qualitative, independent variables represent the nuisance factor, included in the specification of the model in order to make it more realistic. In this type of application, the analysis of covariance technique extends the study of regression analysis to data of more complex structure in which the nature of the regression might be obscured by the effects of the categorical independent variable. In analyzing data in this context, the researcher first removes the effects of the categorical independent variable, and then examines the nature of the relationship between the quantitative variables.

With the third perspective, which we designate as the regression perspective, the covariate(s) and the categorical independent variable(s) are of equal interest and there is often no reason to suspect any causal priority. In cases such as this, the researcher may wish to examine the effect or contribution of each independent variable (both quantitative and qualitative), after adjusting or correcting for the effects of all other independent variables. This perspective is most commonly taken in cases involving observational, rather than experimental data. This analysis is equivalent to regression analysis where the qualitative independent variables are represented by dummy variables.

The perspective adopted by the researcher will usually depend upon the problem context, the type of data employed and, in some cases, the background of the researcher. The two most commonly used perspectives are the experimental and the regression perspectives. Also, it should be noted that the name applied to the analysis may vary depending upon the perspective taken. Those researchers trained in an experimental design tradition usually employ the experimental perspective and label the procedure, analysis of covariance. On the other hand, researchers exposed more often to problems which are not amenable to experimentation usually assume the regression perspective and label the procedure regression analysis with dummy variables.

With this background, a brief discussion of some applications of analysis of covariance is presented before entering into a more technical discussion of the procedure itself.

2. APPLICATIONS OF ANALYSIS OF COVARIANCE

Four applications of analysis of covariance are presented below. The discussion is nontechnical in nature, and intended to provide a sense for the type of situations in which analysis of covariance has been and can be utilized. The applications discussed include both observational and experimental studies.

Application One: Coerciveness and Change

Feierabend and Feierabend (1972) report on an observational study relating the rate of social change to the level of permissiveness-coerciveness of a political regime. The final analysis of the study is a one-way analysis of covariance utilizing data from seventy-six countries over the post World War II period. The dependent variable is the rate of socioeconomic change, a combined rate of change index based on the pooled standard scores of annual measures of change on selected variables (caloric intake, urbanization, radios, and primary education). The categorical independent variable is the degree of permissiveness-coerciveness; three levels based on the composite ratings of three factors (presence of civil rights, toleration of political opposition, and democracy in government) intended to measure the extent to which political and social freedoms are present in a society.

Analysis of covariance was utilized in an effort to adjust the rate of socioeconomic change for the level of development of each country (the covariate), expressed in a modernity index (computed by averaging standard scores on the following indicators: urbanization, gross national product, caloric intake, physicians, newspapers, radios, and telephones). The rationale for this adjustment is the assumption that the more highly developed a country is, the lower the relative change is apt to be. This adjustment is made so as to allow the measurement of the degree to which differences between groups are significant when each case is set statistically equal to every other case on the controlled variable (level of development). This particular application represents an attempt to remove the effects of a disturbing variable (i.e., the bias introduced because the groups were not matched on level of development) in an observational study.

**Application Two:
Partitioning and Perceived Crowding in a Public Space**

Stokols, Smith, and Prostor (1975) report on a field experiment to examine the potential utility of behavioral research for architectural design. They investigated the relationship between a specific aspect of architectural design (method of aerial partitioning) and the perception of crowding. The setting for the research was the waiting area in a southern California office of the Division of Motor Vehicles. Three experimental trials were conducted on successive Mondays, each employing one of three levels of partitioning. The first level involved minimal partitioning in which the floor area was uncluttered and persons waiting for service could form a line in any manner they chose. The second involved a series of ropes and standings which partitioned the area in a maze-like fashion so as to direct the movement of individuals waiting in line. The third method was similar to the second with the exception that five foot high portable partitions were used in place of ropes. The main dependent measures considered in the study were the degree to which subjects felt crowded or uncrowded, and relaxed or tense while waiting in line.

It was suspected that individual differences in subjects would influence reaction to the experimental variable. Therefore, specific characteristics most likely to moderate subjects' reactions were identified. They included items pertaining to the subjects perception of crowding and noise at home, their friendliness towards roommate or family members and the number of persons with whom they shared a bedroom.

Upon exit from the waiting area each subject was asked to complete a questionnaire, which included a series of seven-point bi-polar scales pertaining to the dependent variables. Information on subject characteristics was also obtained. The data were anlayzed using analysis of covariance in the context of a two-way (two variable: method of partitioning and sex) design. A separate analysis was conducted for each dependent variable.

In this application, covariance analysis was employed in conjunction with a field experiment in an effort to statistically control or adjust for individual subject differences. By inclusion of the covariates, the researcher can adjust for those behavioral differences attributable to subject characteristics. This reduces the variability of response within levels of the experimental variable, and therefore, achieves a more accurate experiment.

Application Three:
Comparison of Alternate Teaching Methods

Some experimental studies employ existing (intact) groups which may differ in some important respects. In many instances intact groups offer a more practical approach to a given problem. In such instances, analysis of covariance may be a useful device for performing the statistical analysis because it provides a means both to remove bias attributable to the experimental groups not being matched on some important subject characteristic, and to increase the precision of the experiment. Pasternack and Charen (1969) illustrated the use of analysis of covariance in the comparison of the relative effectiveness of two methods of presenting laboratory experiments to (intact) classes of high school students. The classes differed in previous knowledge of the subject matter and in level of intelligence. It was suspected that these differences might influence the achievement of the students on the evaluative instruments used. Therefore, the scores of the students were statistically adjusted for differences in the auxiliary variables by analysis of covariance.

Operationally, the study consisted of a pretest followed by the experimental manipulation with the same test being given at the completion of the experiment. Also, IQ scores of the students in the classes were obtained. In this case, the posttest score was the dependent variable, type of instruction was the independent categorical variable of primary concern, and the two other independent variables, pretest and IQ scores, were employed as covariates. This particular instance illustrates the use of analysis of covariance in an effort to remove bias which would result because the intact groups were not matched on some relevant variable.

Application Four:
American Occupational Structure

Blau and Duncan (1967), in their study *American Occupational Structure*, illustrate the use of analysis of covariance in the context of an observational study. They considered the problem of relating present occupational status to occupational status of the first job, where occupational status is measured on an interval scale. However, the researchers were concerned that educational level will have an effect on the relationship under investigation. For this specific case, analysis of covariance may be employed to investigate whether or not the slopes (i.e., the nature of the linear relationship between present occupational status and status of first job) are the same for all educational levels. The problem is formulated with present occupational status as the dependent variable, educational level as the categorical independent variable, and occupational status on first job as the continuous independent variable or covariate. Analysis of covariance may be used in this application to detect major patterns of interaction that may be present in the three variable problem. If no interaction is detected, then it will be assumed that the slope, the coefficient relating present occupational status to occupational status of the first job, is constant over occupational levels; in which case, the data may be pooled and a common slope employed. In this particular problem, interest centers on the relationship of the dependent variable and the covariate.

3. PRINCIPAL USES OF ANALYSIS OF COVARIANCE

Problem applications in which analysis of covariance is appropriate are characterized by the presence of a quantitative dependent variable, and both quantitative and qualitative independent variables. A large number of experimental and observational studies meet this criterion. And, even though it has not been frequently applied to problems in the social sciences, analysis of covariance has numerous potential applications for social science research.

The principal uses of analysis of covariance are:

(1) to increase precision in randomized experiments,
(2) to remove bias which may result when test units cannot be assigned at random to experimental conditions,
(3) to remove the effects of disturbing variables in observational studies, and
(4) to fit regressions in the context of multiple classifications.

Increase Precision of Randomized Experiments

In experimental settings considerable effort is usually expended in an attempt to increase the accuracy of the experiment by controlling extraneous variability. Extraneous variability in experiments is typically controlled in one of two ways. The experimenter either applies experimental (direct) control or statistical (indrect) control. Direct control includes such methods as maintaining extraneous variables at constant levels, grouping the objects under study into homogeneous groups (blocks), increasing the uniformity of conditions under which the experiment is run, and increasing the accuracy of the measurements. This type of control is incorporated through the design of experimental procedures.

Indirect (statistical) control relates to the analysis of the experiment rather than its design. Statistical control may be achieved by measuring one or more concomitant variables in addition to the independent variable(s) of primary interest. By partitioning out the amount of variability in the dependent variable accounted for by the concomitant variables, the experimenter is able to more accurately assess the influence of the other independent (experimental) variable(s).

In randomized experiments, the dependent variable, in addition to being influenced by the experimental variable(s), may be subject to the influence of a quantitative independent variable, often reflecting some characteristic of the test unit. In these cases, covariance analysis serves to increase the precision of the experiment by removing the effect of an extraneous source of variance that would otherwise inflate the experimental error. This is similar to the reduction obtained by paring or matching test units.

The gain in precision from the use of the covariance adjustment depends upon the degree of correlation between the covariate and the dependent variable. The higher this correlation, the larger the variation attributable to the covariate, and the more effective the analysis of covariance procedure will be in reducing the error variance.

Remove Bias Due to Nonrandom Assignment of Experimental Test Units

Numerous situations arise in which the researcher finds it unfeasible to randomly assign individual test units to treatment conditions. In these cases a common procedure is to utilize preexisting (intact) groups and to randomly assign treatment levels to these groups. The utilization of analysis of covariance under these conditions may result in two benefits. First, analysis of covariance provides a method to adjust for preexisting differences among the intact groups employed in the experiment. In this respect, analysis of covariance may remove bias attributable to the fact that the intact groups are not similar, or matched, on certain important test unit characteristics. Second, the use of analysis of covariance in these situations may result in the same benefit as in a completely randomized experiment, that is, increase the precision of the experiment by reducing the error variance.

While the use of the analysis of covariance to adjust for preexisting differences among intact groups is very useful in certain instances, it should be used with caution. This caution stems from the fact that when random assignment is not used in forming experimental groups, the results may be subject to difficulties in interpretation. Whereas, in a properly randomized experiment all uncontrolled variables are distributed among the groups in such a way that they can be taken into account with the test of significance employed; this is not necessarily true when intact groups are employed. Therefore, there remains the possibility that some variable has been overlooked that will bias the evaluation of the experiment. The fact that the use of intact groups removes certain safeguards which are assured due to randomization, is pointed out by Lord (1967 and 1969). Lord concludes that when the test units are not randomly assigned to treatment groups, there is no logical nor statistical procedure that can be counted on to make proper allowances for uncontrolled preexisting differences between groups. Also, an inconvenience which often arises with the use of intact groups is that an unequal number of test units are assigned to the various treatment groups. This results in an unbalanced design which may complicate the analysis procedures in certain cases.

When to Use Analysis of Covariance in Experimental Settings

It should be understood that statistical control (e.g., covariance adjustment) and direct experimental control are alternate approaches to achieving the same goal of increasing the precision of an experiment. In some cases it may be convenient to control some variables by direct experimental control and some by statistical control (as is done in the randomized block analysis of covariance to be discussed later). This leads to the question of how to determine when to use covariance analysis.

Analysis of covariance is usually considered appropriate when the following conditions prevail: (1) there are one or more extraneous sources of variation believed to affect the dependent variable; (2) this extraneous source of variation can be measured on an interval (or ratio) scale; (3) the functional form of the relationship between the dependent variable and the extraneous variable(s) is known (a linear relationship is usually assumed); (4) direct experimental control of extraneous sources of variation is either not possible or not feasible; and (5) it is possible to obtain a measure of extraneous variation that does not include effects of the treatment. The fifth criterion is met when; (a) the observations on the covariate are obtained prior to the presentation of the treatments, or (b) the observations on the covariate are obtained after the presentation of the treatments but before the treatments have had an opportunity to affect the covariate, or (c) it can be assumed that the covariate is unaffected by the treatment. If this fifth condition is not satisfied and the covariate is influenced by the treatment, the adjustment made on the dependent variable is biased because some effects attributable to the treatment are eliminated from the dependent variable.

If measurements on the covariate(s) are obtained prior to presentation of treatments, an alternative research strategy is to use the covariate to form homogeneous groups of test units (blocks), and to analyze the data with the appropriate (randomized block design) analysis of variance procedure. In general, direct experimental control is considered preferable to analysis of covariance if an experimenter's principal interest is in reducing the experimental error, rather than removing bias from estimates of treatments effects caused by the use of intact groups. It is important to note that randomized block analysis of variance requires less restrictive assumptions than does covariance analysis. Analysis of covariance assumes that the correct form of regression equation has been fitted, and that the within treatment regression coefficients are homogeneous (the effect of the covariate does not vary over treatment groups). But the randomized block design is essentially a function-free regression that is appropriate even though the relationship between the dependent variable and the extraneous variable is nonlinear. Consequently, if homogeneous blocks can be formed, one need not worry about knowing the functional relationship between the blocking variable and the dependent variable. However, the interaction of blocks and treatment levels is assumed to be zero in most randomized block designs. This assumption is analogous to the assumption of homogeneity of regression coefficients in a covariance analysis.

Remove Bias in Observational Studies

In observational studies, naturally occurring groups are analyzed. With these groups it is recognized that differences in the dependent variable may occur due to differences in certain characteristics (variables) of the groups which are not of primary concern to the analysis. If analysis of variance is conducted without considering these characteristics, the results may be biased. In those cases where the disturbing variables are quantitative (interval- or ratio-scaled), analysis of covariance may be employed in an effort to remove the bias introduced because the groups have not been matched on these disturbing variables. In other words, differences may exist in these disturbing variables from group to group, and covariance analysis provides a means to statistically adjust the dependent variable for these preexisting differences. Also, in cases where the groups do not differ on the disturbing variables and there is no danger of bias, the covariance adjustment may act to increase the precision of the analysis in the same manner as in a randomized experiment.

Observational studies have a similarity to experimental studies employing intact groups. With experimental studies and intact groups, one is unable to randomly assign test units to treatments, however, one typically insures that treatments are randomly assigned into experimental groups. Observational studies utilize natural intact groups in which no random assignment may be made by the researcher. Therefore, the problems that may exist when using intact groups in experimental settings are also present and possibly compounded in observational settings. Typically, the way to ascertain whether these problems exist or not, is to investigate the degree of multicollinearity (amount of linear association among the independent variables) which exist within the observational data. If this collinearity is high it may be difficult or impossible to statistically separate the impact of the various independent variables on the dependent variable.

Regression with Multiple Classifications

In other situations, usually nonexperimental, interest of the researcher centers on the relationship between two or more quantitative variables; but concern exists with regard to the possible effects of some qualitative (categorical) variable upon this relationship. That is, the group to which the test units belong, or the classification of which they are a part, may moderate the nature of the relationship between the quantitative variables so that it will differ across groups or classifications. In cases such as this, analysis of covariance may be employed. In this analysis the researcher must first establish that there is no interaction between the covariate and the categorical independent variable. If an interaction is shown to exist, it warns the researcher that the relationship between the covariate and dependent variable varies over the levels of the categorical independent variable and that separate, individual analyses must be conducted for each level of the categorical independent variable. If the interaction is not statistically significant, it supports the assumption of constant slope, and the data for all levels of the categorical independent variable may be analyzed together within the context of the analysis of covariance model.

4. STATISTICAL PROCEDURES FOR ANALYSIS OF COVARIANCE FOR A ONE-WAY LAYOUT

Introduction

A one-way layout describes any context involving a single qualitative independent variable, with any number of levels, and one or more covariates (quantitative independent variables). The one-way layout is common to both experimental and observational studies. In randomized experiments, the one-way layout is analogous to the completely randomized design, where test units are randomly assigned to treatment levels of a single qualitative independent variable. Random experiments provide a strong basis for hypothesis testing, that is, they allow the rigorous testing of causal hypotheses, and represent the most desirable, though sometimes unattainable, conditions for hypothesis testing. In other experiments, where random assignment of test units is not feasible, preexisting groups are used and the treatment levels are randomly assigned to these intact groups. This type of experimental design is also a one-way layout, as long as it includes a single qualitative independent variable; but it does not, in general, lend itself to as strong a basis of hypothesis testing as does the completely randomized experiment. Observational studies, involving multiple groups, also come under the heading of the one-way layout. With observational studies, the test units are not randomly assigned to groups nor are the treatments randomly assigned to groups by the researcher, and this type of study is not as rigorous as experimental designs in establishing causal relationships between variables. Furthermore, as in experiments with intact groups, it is more difficult to eliminate the possibility that the group membership of a test unit has been influenced by the co-variate or vice versa, which would bias the results.

As previously mentioned, three distinct problem perspectives may be employed in conjunction with analysis of covariance. Here we address the analysis procedures for one-way layouts associated with all three perspectives. However, primary consideration is given to the experimental perspective, which includes those cases, both observational and experimental, in which primary interest is in the effect of a single qualitative independent variable on the dependent variable and the covariates are considered nuisance variables. (It is noted that in this and subsequent sections of this paper a basic knowledge of analysis of variance and regression analysis is assumed. Also, all discussion of experimental designs that follows considers only fixed effects models. Consequently, it is *not* assumed that the treatment levels are a random selection of all possible treatment levels, so findings cannot be generalized to treatment levels other than those particular levels included in the analysis.)

Covariance Model

For the one-way layout, the covariance model considers the observed value of the dependent variable to be influenced by the effect of the particular treatment level or group from which the observation comes, and the values of the concomitant variables (covariates). Verbally, an additive model representing this situation is:

$$
\begin{bmatrix} \text{Observed value} \\ \text{of dependent} \\ \text{variables} \end{bmatrix} = [\text{constant}] + \begin{bmatrix} \text{effect of} \\ \text{treatment} \\ \text{level or group} \end{bmatrix} + \begin{bmatrix} \text{effect} \\ \text{of} \\ \text{covariate} \end{bmatrix} + \begin{bmatrix} \text{resi-} \\ \text{dual} \\ \text{effect} \end{bmatrix}
$$

Algegraically, the analysis of covariance model for the one-way layout with one covariate is represented as:

$$Y_{ij} = u + \tau_i + \beta(X_{ij} - \overline{X}) + e_{ij}; \quad i=1,\ldots,k; \quad j=1,\ldots,n_i; \qquad [1]$$

where Y_{ij} is the observed value of the dependent variable for the jth observation within the ith group or treatment level, u is the true mean effect, τ_i is the effect due to the ith group or level of the categorical independent variable (treatment) with $\Sigma n_i \tau_i = 0$, β is the (regression) coefficient representing the average effect of a one unit change in the covariate on the dependent variable, X_{ij} is the observed value of the covariate, $\overline{X}$ is the general mean of the covariate, e_{ij} is a random error which is normally and independently distributed with mean zero and variance σ^2, k is the number of groups, and n_i is the number of observations in group i. The term $(X_{ij} - \overline{X})$ is used rather than X_{ij} so that the constant term of the model will be the grand mean of the dependent variable.

An explicit examination of the assumptions underlying the analysis of covariance model and the consequences of violating those assumptions is presented in the Appendix. Also, it is noted that the above model and the discussion that follows are applicable whether there are an equal or unequal number of observations in each group. However, for convenience of exposition the subscript on n_i will usually be dropped and $\sum_{i=1}^{k} n_i$ will be designated as N.

Completely Randomized Design

The term "completely randomized design" is used here in a broad sense and refers to those contexts, both experimental and observational, where interest centers on detecting differences in the dependent variable over the various levels of a single qualitative independent variable, which may represent distinct naturally occurring groups of observations or levels of an experimental treatment. The problem perspective assumed here is that which has previously been labled the experimental perspective, in which interest centers on the relationship between the qualitative independent variable and the dependent variable with the covariate, or quantitative independent variable, considered as a nuisance variable. Under this perspective, covariance analysis provides a means to adjust the dependent variable for the value of the covariate for each observation. This should allow more precise information on the treatment or group effects to be obtained. This is accomplished by reducing the error variance (i.e., subtracting out the effect of the covariate) and/or by adjusting the group means on the dependent variable for differences in the mean values of the covariate for the respective groups.

The adjustment for the covariate may be made in any of several different ways. In given instances the appropriate form of the adjustment is determined from prior knowledge about the relationship between the dependent variable and the covariate. However, in a large number of applications no strong evidence exists to indicate the form of the adjustment, in these cases the adjustment is usually assumed to amount to some scalar multiple of the covariate. Although the form of the adjustment need not be linear, only the linear case will be considered here. Furthermore, only one covariate will be considered in the following discussion. (For a discussion of multiple covariates refer to Kirk [1968] or Winer [1971].)

Considering equation 1, the dependent variable may be adjusted for the covariate as follows:

$$Y_{ij(adj)} = Y_{ij} - \beta(X_{ij} - \bar{X}) = u + \tau_i + e_{ij} \qquad [2]$$

where $Y_{ij(adj)}$ is the value of the dependent variable adjusted for the covariate. Since, as in analysis of variance, the usual purpose of analysis of covariance within the experimental perspective is to test the hypothesis that group means are equal, an obvious approach would be to conduct analysis of variance on the adjusted scores, $Y_{ij(adj)}$. If β were known, this would be an appropriate approach to the problem. However, β must be estimated from the data and that estimate is made by utilizing all data observed under all treatment levels. Under these conditions, the adjusted treatment means are not independent of each other, and the assumptions necessary for establishing the ratio of mean squares as an F-distribution are violated. Therefore, some alternative approach must be employed. Consistent with the above rationale, this alternate approach should yield the appropriate sum of squares and mean square terms (necessary for the F-test), which are adjusted for the covariate. One such approach is described below.

If one wishes to predict the value of a particular observation on the dependent variable with knowledge of the sample mean for the dependent variable and the value of the associated covariate, but with no knowledge of which group or treatment is associated with each observation, how would one proceed? A reasonable approach would be to use the value of the sample mean adjusted by the value of the covariate. Specifically, the model used to yield this estimate would be,

$$Y'_{ij} = \bar{Y} + b_T(X_{ij} - \bar{X}) \qquad [3]$$

where;

Y'_{ij} = the predicted score for observation j in group i,

$\overline{Y}$ = the grand (sample) mean of the dependent variable,

X_{ij} = the value of the covariate for observation j in group i,

$\overline{X}$ = the grand (sample) mean of covariate, and

b_T = the estimated coefficient for the covariate.

It is noted that the predicted score, Y'_{ij}, represents that portion of the dependent variable accounted for by the covariate, i.e., with knowledge of only the value of the covariate.

At this point a question may arise as to how one might obtain an estimate for the coefficient of the covariate term. A close look reveals that equation 3 can be viewed as a simple regression model with $(Y_{ij} - \overline{Y})$ as a dependent variable and $(X_{ij} - \overline{X})$ as the independent variable. It is a relatively easy matter to obtain b_T by the method of least squares. b_T will be referred to as the overall regression coefficient and is computed:

$$b_T = \frac{\displaystyle\sum_{i=1}^{k}\sum_{j=1}^{n} (X_{ij} - \overline{X})(Y_{ij} - \overline{Y})}{\displaystyle\sum_{i=1}^{k}\sum_{j=1}^{n} (X_{ij} - \overline{X})^2} . \qquad [4]$$

With this estimate of b_T, the total sum of squares of Y adjusted for the covariate (and grand mean), which is also the sum of squared residuals about the regression line, may be computed. It is designated as $T_{yy(adj)}$ and is computed as follows:

$$T_{yy(adj)} = \sum_{i=1}^{k}\sum_{j=1}^{n} (Y_{ij} - Y'_{ij})^2$$

$$= \sum_{i=1}^{k}\sum_{j=1}^{n} [Y_{ij} - \overline{Y} - b_T(X_{ij} - \overline{X})]^2$$

$$= \sum_{i=1}^{k}\sum_{j=1}^{n} (Y_{ij} - \overline{Y})^2 + b_T^2 \sum_{i=1}^{k}\sum_{j=1}^{n} (X_{ij} - \overline{X})^2$$

$$- 2b_T \sum_{i=1}^{k}\sum_{j=1}^{n} (X_{ij} - \overline{X})(Y_{ij} - \overline{Y}).$$

But from equation 4,

$$\sum_{i=1}^{k} \sum_{j=1}^{n} (X_{ij} - \bar{X})(Y_{ij} - \bar{Y}) = b_T \sum_{i=1}^{k} \sum_{j=1}^{n} (X_{ij} - \bar{X})^2$$

therefore,

$$T_{yy(adj)} = \sum_{i=1}^{k} \sum_{j=1}^{n} (Y_{ij} - \bar{Y})^2 - b_T^2 \sum_{i=1}^{k} \sum_{j=1}^{n} (X_{ij} - \bar{X})^2. \qquad [5]$$

This sum of squares represents variation among the values of the dependent variable attributable to the group or treatment effect and the residual effect, but which is *not* associated with the linear regression of Y on X.

It is noted that the right hand side of equation 5 consists of two terms. The first, $\sum\sum (Y_{ij} - \bar{Y})^2$, is the total sum of squares of Y (adjusted for the grand mean) not adjusted for the covariate. This term is designated T_{yy} and is referred to as the total sum of squares of Y. The second term; $b_T^2 \sum\sum (X_{ij} - \bar{X})^2$ or $b_T^2 T_{xx}$, where $T_{xx} = \sum\sum (X_{ij} - \bar{X})^2$ is the total sum of squares of X; represents an adjustment that is made to the unadjusted total sum of squares of Y which removes linear effects of the covariate. This adjustment will always reduce the sum of squares for Y as long as b_T does not equal 0. Consequently, the total adjusted sum of squares of Y, $T_{yy(adj)}$, is sometimes called the reduced sum of squares. By defining $T_{xy} = \sum\sum (X_{ij} - \bar{X})(Y_{ij} - \bar{Y})$, the sum of squares for the cross product of X and Y, the adjusted total sum of squares is expressed, using abbreviated notation, as,

$$T_{yy(adj)} = T_{yy} - b_T^2 T_{xx} = T_{yy} - T_{xy}^2 / T_{xx}. \qquad [6]$$

The degrees of freedom for $T_{yy(adj)}$ are $N - 2$. One additional degree of freedom, as compared to completely randomized analysis of variance, has been lost because of the linear restriction imposed on the sum of squares, i.e., deviations from the regression line rather than from the sample mean are used to compute the adjusted total sum of squares.

The variation in Y associated with the error term in the covariance model is specified by the adjusted within group sum of squares, $E_{yy(adj)}$, and is the sum of the squared deviations of the observed value of the dependent variable from the value predicted with knowledge of the associated group or treatment level and the covariate. This predicted value is computed as follows:

$$Y'_{j|i} = \bar{Y}_i + b_w(X_{ij} - \bar{X}_i) \qquad [7]$$

where $\bar{Y}_i$ and $\bar{X}_i$ are the means of Y_{ij} and X_{ij}, respectively for group i, and b_w is an estimate of β in equation 1 obtained by estimating the simple regression model with $(Y_{ij} - \bar{Y}_i)$ as the dependent variable and $(X_{ij} - \bar{X}_i)$ as the independent variable. Computationally, b_w is expressed:

$$b_w = \frac{\sum_{i=1}^{k} \sum_{j=1}^{n} (X_{ij} - \bar{X}_i)(Y_{ij} - \bar{Y}_i)}{\sum_{i=1}^{k} \sum_{j=1}^{n} (X_{ij} - \bar{X}_i)^2} \qquad [8]$$

and is referred to as the pooled within class regression coefficient.

With this estimate of b_w, $E_{yy(adj)}$ is computed as follows:

$$E_{yy(adj)} = \sum_{i=1}^{k} \sum_{j=1}^{n} (Y_{ij} - Y'_{ij})^2$$

$$= \sum_{i=1}^{k} \sum_{j=1}^{n} [Y_{ij} - \bar{Y}_i - b_w(X_{ij} - \bar{X}_i)]^2$$

$$= \sum_{i=1}^{k} \sum_{j=1}^{n} (Y_{ij} - \bar{Y}_i)^2 + b_w^2 \sum_{i=1}^{k} \sum_{j=1}^{n} (X_{ij} - \bar{X}_i)^2$$

$$- 2b_w \sum_{i=1}^{k} \sum_{j=1}^{n} (X_{ij} - \bar{X}_i)(Y_{ij} - \bar{Y}_i).$$

But from equation 8,

$$\sum_{i=1}^{k} \sum_{j=1}^{n} (Y_{ij} - \bar{Y}_i)(X_{ij} - \bar{X}_i) = b_w \sum_{i=1}^{k} \sum_{j=1}^{n} (X_{ij} - \bar{X}_i)^2$$

therefore,

$$E_{yy(adj)} = \sum_{i=1}^{k} \sum_{j=1}^{n} (Y_{ij} - \bar{Y}_i)^2 - b_w^2 \sum_{i=1}^{k} \sum_{j=1}^{n} (X_{ij} - \bar{X}_i)^2. \qquad [9]$$

This sum of squares represents variation among the values of the dependent variable attributable to the residual effect *only*.

It is noted that, as with the adjusted total sum of squares of Y, the adjusted within group sum of squares consists of two components: $E_{yy} = \Sigma\Sigma (Y_{ij} - \bar{Y}_i)^2$, the unadjusted within group sum of squares of Y; and, $b_w^2 E_{xx}$, where $E_{xx} = \Sigma\Sigma (X_{ij} - \bar{X}_i)^2$ is the within group sum of squares of X, which represents an adjustment that removes the linear effect of the covariate. By defining $E_{xy} = \Sigma\Sigma (X_{ij} - \bar{X}_i)(Y_{ij} - \bar{Y}_i)$, the within group sum of squares for the cross product of X and Y, the adjusted within group sum of squares is expressed:

$$E_{yy(adj)} = E_{yy} - b_w^2 E_{xx} = E_{yy} - E_{xy}^2 / E_{xx}. \qquad [10]$$

The degrees of freedom for $E_{yy(adj)}$ are N-k-1. Again, one degree of freedom has been lost because of the linear restriction imposed, which results in the deviations being computed from the regression line.

The adjusted total sum of squares, $T_{yy(adj)}$, represents variation due to the treatment or group effect plus the residual effect; and the adjusted within group sum of squares, $E_{yy(adj)}$, represents variation due to only the residual effect. Therefore, the adjusted between group sum of squares of Y, $B_{yy(adj)}$, which represents variation due only to the treatment or group effect may be computed by subtraction,

$$B_{yy(adj)} = T_{yy(adj)} - E_{yy(adj)}. \qquad [11]$$

The degrees of freedom associated with $B_{yy(adj)}$, which are equal to the difference in the degrees of freedom of the terms in equation 11, are (N-2)-(N-k-1) = k-1.

At this point, the reader may be curious as to why the adjusted between group sum of squares is computed by subtraction rather than by a procedure analogous to that used in computing the adjusted total and adjusted within group sums of squares. The reason is that in cases where group effects exist the use of this second method would result in a covariance adjustment which would also remove a portion of the variation attributable to the treatment or group effect. This would be unsatisfactory, and therefore, the approach given by equation 11 is used.

With the computation of the three adjusted sums of squares, the null hypothesis of no group effects, i.e., $\tau_i = 0$ for all i, can be tested. As in analysis of variance, an F-statistic is computed. It is of the form,

$$F = \frac{B_{yy(adj)}/(k-1)}{E_{yy(adj)}/(N-k-1)} .$$
[12]

Under the null hypothesis (and the model assumptions) this ratio has an F-distribution with degrees of freedom k-1 and N-k-1. In terms of predicted scores, this test is equivalent to testing the hypothesis that scores predicted using equation 3 fit the data as well as scores predicted using equation 7. That is, the test examines whether knowledge of group membership significantly adds to the prediction of the dependent variable. (Refer to pages 45-49 for a more detailed discussion of the correspondence between hypothesis testing and comparison of alternate models.)

A summary of the computational formulae associated with the analysis of covariance for the completely randomized design is presented in Table 1.

The F-statistic given by equation 12 is only a summary measure which indicates if any significant group differences in the dependent variable exist. If significant differences are present, one naturally wants to investigate the nature of these differences. Therefore, when the F-ratio is significant it is customary to compute the group means adjusted for the covariate to aid in the interpretation of the results. The adjusted group means are computed as follows:

$$\bar{Y}_{i(adj)} = \bar{Y}_i - b(\bar{X}_i - \bar{X}); \quad i=1, \ldots, k,$$
[13]

where $b = b_w$, is the unbiased estimate of β in equation 1 calculated from the error sums of squares and cross products, as shown in equation 8. What this adjustment does is eliminate the effect of the covariate from the group means which allows for more meaningful interpretation.

The comparison of group means and the interpretation of the statistical analysis are considered in more detail immediately following the next section.

TESTING β

Accompanying the covariance model are certain implicit assumptions concerning the coefficient of the covariate. Two of these assumptions,

TABLE 1
Analysis of Covariance for Completely Randomized Design

Source of Variation	Sum of Squares and Cross Products			Adjusted Sum of Squares	Degrees of Freedom	Adjusted Mean Square	Expected Mean Square	F-Ratio
	XX	XY	YY					
Treatment/ Group	--	--	--	$B_{YY(ADJ)}$	$K-1$	$\dfrac{B_{YY(ADJ)}}{K-1}$	$\sigma^2_{\epsilon\mid\beta} + \dfrac{\Sigma N_I T_I^2}{K-1}$	$\dfrac{MST_{(ADJ)}}{MSE_{(ADJ)}}$
Error	E_{XX}	E_{XY}	E_{YY}	$E_{YY(ADJ)}$	$N-K-1$	$\dfrac{E_{YY(ADJ)}}{N-K-1}$	$\sigma^2_{\epsilon\mid\beta}$	
Total	T_{XX}	T_{XY}	T_{YY}	$T_{YY(ADJ)}$	$N-2$			

$E_{xx} = \Sigma\Sigma(X_{ij} - \bar{X}_i)^2$

$E_{xy} = \Sigma\Sigma(X_{ij} - \bar{X}_i)(Y_{ij} - \bar{Y}_i)$

$E_{yy} = \Sigma\Sigma(Y_{ij} - \bar{Y}_i)^2$

$T_{xx} = \Sigma\Sigma(X_{ij} - \bar{X})^2$

$T_{xy} = \Sigma\Sigma(X_{ij} - \bar{X})(Y_{ij} - \bar{Y})$

$T_{yy} = \Sigma\Sigma(Y_{ij} - \bar{Y})^2$

$E_{yy(adj)} = E_{yy} - E_{xy}^2/E_{xx}$

$T_{yy(adj)} = T_{yy} - T_{xy}^2/T_{xx}$

$B_{yy(adj)} = T_{yy(adj)} - E_{yy(adj)}$

$b_w = E_{xy}/E_{xx}$

which should be verified before the results of the covariance analysis are used, are:

(1) the effect, or impact, of the covariate on the dependent variable is the same for all levels of the categorical independent variable, and

(2) the coefficient is nonzero.

Sufficient information is available through the computations associated with the analysis of covariance model to test each of these assumptions. (Some consequences of violating the above and other assumptions are discussed in the Appendix.)

In analysis of covariance, an assumption underlying the adjustment of the within group sum of squares is that the within group regression coefficients are equal for all groups. Consequently, before the analysis of covariance results are interpreted one should test the hypothesis that these coefficients are equal. An analogy might be drawn here to two-way analysis of variance. In two-way analysis of variance the first test made is usually the test for an interaction effect. The reason for making this test first, is that, if the two independent variables produce different results, when acting in combination, than would be expected on the basis of the separate effects, then it makes very little sense, theoretically, to study the effects of one independent variable while not controlling for the other. In other words, the relationship between one independent variable and the dependent variable differs according to the value of the other independent variable; consequently, the relationships should be studied separately within each category of the other independent variable. A similar problem is faced in analysis of covariance. If the slopes, within group regression coefficients, differ significantly across groups, it is inappropriate to use the covariance model (equation 1) which assumes a constant slope. We should, in that case, consider a more complex model having a unique slope for each group.

A test for the homogeneity of regression coefficients is given by

$$F = \frac{(E_{yy(adj)} - S_1)/(k-1)}{S_1/(N - 2k)} , \qquad [14]$$

where $E_{yy(adj)}$ has been previously defined as the adjusted within group sum of squares (i.e., the sum of squared deviations about the regression line assuming a common regression coefficient over all groups), and S_1 is the sum of squared deviations about the within class regression lines, each with unique slope depending upon the particular treatment level. Algebraically,

$$S_1 = E_{yy} - \sum_{i=1}^{k} b_{w_i}^2 E_{xx_i}, \qquad [15]$$

where $b_{w_i} = E_{xy_i}/E_{xx_i}$ is the within class regression coefficient for group i, $E_{xy_i} = \Sigma_j(X_{ij} - \overline{X}_i)(Y_{ij} - \overline{Y}_i)$ is the within group sum of squares for the cross product of X and Y for group i, and $E_{xx_i} = \Sigma_j(X_{ij} - \overline{X}_i)^2$ is the within group sum of squares of X for group i. Making substitutions, equation 14 becomes:

$$F = \frac{\left(\sum_{i=1}^{k} b_{w_i}^2 E_{xx_i} - b_w^2 E_{xx}\right)/(k-1)}{\left(E_{yy} - \sum_{i=1}^{k} b_{w_i}^2 E_{xx_i}\right)/(N - 2k)} \cdot, \qquad [16]$$

which, under the hypothesis of homogeneity of the within class regression, is distributed as the F-distribution with k-1 and N-2k degrees of freedom. In this test one must be especially worried about committing a type II error, i.e., accepting the null hypothesis of no difference when it is false, so a numerically large level of significance (α = .10 or larger) is recommended.

It is evident from the formulation of the covariance model that the coefficient of the covariate is assumed to be nonzero. If this were not the case, there would be no benefit to complicating the analysis by the inclusion of the covariate. In certain instances the researcher may wish to test this assumption. In testing this assumption, the null hypothesis is that β equals zero. The validity of this null hypothesis is tested using the F-ratio,

$$F = \left[\frac{E_{xy}^2}{E_{yy}E_{xx} - E_{xy}^2}\right] \cdot (N-k-1), \qquad [17]$$

which, under the null hypothesis, is distributed as the F-distribution, with 1 and N-k-1 degrees of freedom.

COMPARISONS AMONG MEANS

Many studies involve more than two groups or treatment levels. In such studies, a significant F-ratio for group or treatment effects indicates that at least one of the groups differs from another, but not which one or ones. Therefore, additional analysis is usually undertaken to determine which pairs or combinations of group means are significantly different. With analysis of covariance these comparisons are made with the adjusted group means as calculated by equation 13.

A comparison between two group means is made by considering the differences between them, e.g., $\bar{Y}_1 - \bar{Y}_2$, and testing whether that difference is significantly different from zero. A comparison may also involve more than two means. This can be done, for example, by averaging two means and then comparing this average with a third mean. This procedure could give rise to the difference, $(\bar{Y}_1 - \bar{Y}_2)/2 - \bar{Y}_3$. It is evident that the number of possible pairwise and nonpairwise comparisons among group means increases markedly as the number of groups increase.

In general, a comparison among k means takes the form of a linear combination, or weighted sum of means (referred to as a contrast) for which the coefficients, or weights, sum to zero but are not all equal to zero. Algebraically, a contrast is expressed:

$$C = \sum_{i=1}^{k} c_i \bar{Y}_i = c_1 \bar{Y}_1 + c_2 \bar{Y}_2 + \ldots + c_k \bar{Y}_k,, \qquad [18]$$

where

$$\sum_{i=1}^{k} c_i = 0.$$

In terms of this algebraic formulation, the comparison between the two group means, $\bar{Y}_1$ and $\bar{Y}_2$, mentioned in the preceding paragraph is equivalent to setting c_1 equal to $+1$, c_2 equal to -1, and all other c_i equal to zero.

Mean comparisons may be classified as orthogonal or non-orthogonal, and as a priori or a posteriori. Two comparisons among k means are said to be orthogonal to each other if they utilize nonoverlapping pieces of information. A maximum of k-1 mutually orthogonal comparisons are possible in the analysis containing k groups or treatment levels, though the k-1 comparisons are not unique. Another way of viewing orthogonal comparisons is that any treatment/group sum of squares with k−1 degrees of freedom can be divided into k−1 orthogonal components which are additive, i.e., sum to equal the treatment/group sum of squares, and correspond to an orthogonal comparison. Mathematically, two contrasts, C_1 and C_2, are considered orthogonal if

$$\sum_{i=1}^{k} c_{1i} c_{2i}/n_i = 0,$$

where c_{ji} is the coefficient of the ith group mean in the jth contrast and n_i is the number of observations in group i.

A priori or planned comparisons are those which are specified prior to conducting the anlaysis. In experimental studies these usually involve a specific set of hypotheses that the experiment is designed to test. Those comparisons developed *after* conducting the initial analysis, for "exploring" the data, are referred to as a posteriori or post hoc comparisons. While it is usually considered "nice" to use a priori orthogonal comparisons, the choice should be dictated by the type and purpose of the study. The remainder of this section considers a limited number of statistical comparisons. For further discussion the reader is referred to Kirk (Ch. 3, 1968).

A Priori Orthogonal Comparisons. The preceding discussion considered the form of mean comparisons but not the statistical testing of these comparisons. In testing a comparison, the null hypothesis is that the value of the contrast is zero. For example, in the previously considered comparison involving two means, $C = 1\overline{Y}_1 - 1\overline{Y}_2$, the null hypothesis is that the population mean for group one (u_1) minus the population mean for group two (u_2) is zero. (The alternate hypothesis for this test is $u_1 - u_2 \neq 0$.) Within the context of the completely randomized analysis of covariance model, the null hypothesis, in case of planned orthogonal comparisons, may be tested using the t-statistic,

$$t = \frac{\Sigma c_i \overline{Y}_{i(adj)}}{\sqrt{MSE_{(adj)}[\Sigma(c_i^2/n_i) + [\Sigma c_i(\overline{X}_i - \overline{X})]^2/E_{xx}]}}, \qquad [19]$$

with N−k−1 degrees of freedom.

It is noted that when a large number of mean comparisons (multiple comparisons) are made, the probability of obtaining at least one significant comparison, due strictly to chance, can become large. Many researchers have investigated this problem and, as a result, various procedures have been devised which provide for a given α-level over a collection of comparisons. This naturally results in a much lower α-level on any given comparison within the collection. However, according to Kirk (1968: 78), "for planned orthogonal comparisons, contemporary practice in the behavioral sciences favors setting the type I error probability level at α for each comparison. For planned and unplanned nonorthogonal comparisons it is suggested that the type I error probability should be set at α for the collection of comparisons."

A Posteriori Nonorthogonal Comparisons. In many situations the researcher is not sufficiently knowledgeable concerning the effect of the independent variable to a priori specify the appropriate mean comparisons. However, if the overall F-test leads to the rejection of the null hypothesis of no treatment/group effects, the researcher is usually interested in further "exploring" the data in an effort to uncover the sources of the treatment/gorup effect. In such cases of unplanned mean comparisons it is usually recommended that a procedure be employed which maintains a specified α-level for the entire collection of comparisons. Two such procedures are discussed here (Kirk, 1968:472): Tukey's HSD (honestly significant difference) test, sometimes referred to as the "w" procedure, and Scheffe's test.

Tukey's HSD test was designed for making *all pairwise* mean comparisons. The test statistic, in the case of an equal number of observations per group is computed

$$q = \frac{c_i \bar{Y}_{i(adj)} + c_j \bar{Y}_{j(adj)}}{\sqrt{\dfrac{MSE_{(adj)}}{n} \left[1 + \dfrac{B_{xx}}{(k-1)E_{xx}} \right]}}, \qquad [20]$$

where q is compared to q-critical, for k means and $N-k-1$ degrees of freedom, obtained from the distribution of the studentized range statistic (tables for q are reproduced in Kirk [1968]). In the case of unequal cell sizes an approximate statistic can be obtained by substituting n* for n where,

$$n^* = k / \Sigma(1/n_i).$$

Scheffe's test is recommended for *only nonpairwise* mean comparison's since it is less sensitive for pairwise comparisons than Tukey's test. The test statistic is computed:

$$F = \frac{[\Sigma c_i \bar{Y}_{i(adj)}]^2}{MSE_{(adj)}\left[1 + \frac{B_{xx}}{(k-1)E_{xx}}\right]\left[\Sigma(c_i^2/n_i)\right]} \cdot \frac{1}{(k-1)}, \qquad [21]$$

and compared to the tabulated F value with k and N-k-1 degrees of freedom.

NUMERIC EXAMPLE FOR COMPLETELY RANDOMIZED DESIGN

The country of Finland is divided into a large number of political sub-divisions called municipalities. The State owned liquor company has a monopoly on wholesale and package store liquor sales, and has the sole authority to grant liquor licenses for restaurants. For centuries there has been a law that liquor can be sold and/or commercially served only in the urban municipalities. This law, however, was recently (at least temporarily) repealed, and the State liquor monopoly wished to determine whether selling liquor in rural municipalities would have a negative impact.

A key consideration for decision makers was whether the establishment of a liquor store, either alone or with a licensed restaurant, would significantly affect the number of traffic accidents in the rural municipalities. New liquor stores and licensed restaurants were established in rural municipalities at approximately the same time during early summer. Twelve rural municipalities, four where only a package store was licensed, four where both a restaurant and package store were licensed and four where no store or restaurant was licensed, were included in the study. Traffic accident records were obtained for the twelve months prior to the establishment of the liquor stores, and for the twelve months after the establishment of the stores.

The study, as described above, could be either an observational or experimental study depending upon the amount of control the State liquor monopoly had in deciding which municipalities would be licensed. An experimental study would have resulted if the twelve rural municipalities were randomly assigned to the three groups. On the other hand, it would be an observational study if applications for the various types of licensing were processed in the normal manner and, after the appropriate licensing had been obtained, four municipalities with each type of licensing were selected for inclusion in the study.

It was not considered appropriate to use the change (algebric difference between the before and after measures) in traffic accidents as the dependent

TABLE 2
Data for Completely Randomized Design:
Traffic Accidents During the Test Period (Y) and
Traffic Accidents During Preceding Year (X)

| | TYPE OF LIQUOR LICENSING (TREATMENTS OR GROUPS) | | | | | |
| | CONTROL (GROUP 1) | | PACKAGE STORE ONLY (GROUP 2) | | RESTAURANT AND PACKAGE STORE (GROUP 3) | |
	X	Y	X	Y	X	Y
OBSERVED VALUES	190	177	252	226	206	226
	261	225	228	196	239	229
	194	167	240	198	217	215
	217	176	246	206	177	188
MEAN	215.50	186.25	241.50	206.50	209.75	214.50

SAMPLE MEANS X = 222.25   Y = 202.42

variable, because it was well known that there was a decreasing trend in traffic accidents due to less driving per resident, caused by a substantial increase in gasoline prices during this time period. Consequently, it was decided that the after measure would be used as the dependent variable and the before measure as a covariate.

The setting described above represents a completely randomized design with the number of traffic accidents per ten thousand population during the test period as the dependent variable, the number of traffic accidents per ten thousand population during the preceding period as the covariate, and the type of liquor licensing as the categorical independent variable. This categorical independent variable has three levels; (1) no liquor available (control level), (2) package store only, and (3) restaurant licensing and package store. The data resulting from this study are presented in Table 2.

The primary purpose of the study is to determine the impact of liquor licensing on traffic accidents in the rural municipalities. In a statistical framework, the objective is to test the hypothesis that $\tau_i = 0$ for all i, i.e., all three levels of liquor licensing have equal impact on the dependent variable. An α-level of .05 is selected for this test and most subsequent tests. This hypothesis is tested with an F-ratio (equation 12). The F-ratio requires the calculation of $B_{yy(adj)}$ and $E_{yy(adj)}$, the adjusted between group sum of squares of Y, and the adjusted within group sum of squares of Y, respectively. But $B_{yy(adj)}$ is obtained by subtraction (equation 11) and requires calculation of $T_{yy(adj)}$, the adjusted total sum of squares of Y.

The formulae for computing $T_{yy(adj)}$ and $E_{yy(adj)}$ are given by equations 6 and 10, respectively, and require the calculation of the following six terms:

$$T_{xx} = \sum_{i=1}^{3} \sum_{j=1}^{4} (X_{ij} - \bar{X})^2 = \text{total sum of squares of X}$$

$$= (190 - 222.25)^2 + (261 - 222.25)^2 + \ldots + (177 - 222.25)^2$$

$$= 7784.25,$$

$$T_{xy} = \sum_{i=1}^{3} \sum_{j=1}^{4} (X_{ij} - \bar{X})(Y_{ij} - \bar{Y}) = \begin{array}{l} \text{total sum of squares for the} \\ \text{cross product of X and Y} \end{array}$$

$$= (190 - 222.25)(177 - 202.42) + (261 - 222.25)(225 - 202.42)$$

$$+ \ldots + (177 - 222.25)(188 - 202.42)$$

$$= 4153.75,$$

$$T_{yy} = \sum_{i=1}^{3} \sum_{j=1}^{4} (Y_{ij} - \bar{Y})^2 = \text{total sum of squares of Y}$$

$$= (177 - 202.42)^2 + (225 - 202.42)^2 + \ldots + (188 - 202.42)^2$$

$$= 5366.92,$$

$$E_{xx} = \sum_{i=1}^{3} \sum_{j=1}^{4} (X_{ij} - \bar{X}_i)^2 = \text{within group sum of squares of X}$$

$$= (190 - 215.50)^2 + (261 - 215.50)^2 + \ldots + (177 - 209.75)^2$$

$$= 5494.75,$$

$$E_{xy} = \sum_{i=1}^{3} \sum_{j=1}^{4} (X_{ij} - \bar{X}_i)(Y_{ij} - \bar{Y}_i) = \text{within group sum of squares for the cross product of X and Y}$$

$$= (190 - 215.50)(177 - 186.25) + (261 - 215.50)(225 - 186.25)$$

$$+ \ldots + (177 - 209.75)(188 - 214.50)$$

$$= 4005.67,$$

$$E_{yy} = \sum_{i=1}^{3} \sum_{j=1}^{4} (Y_{ij} - \bar{Y}_i)^2 = \text{within group sum of squares of Y}$$

$$= (177 - 186.25)^2 + (225 - 186.25)^2 + \ldots + (188 - 214.50)^2$$

$$= 3670.75.$$

Given these six terms, the adjusted total, within and between group sums of squares ($T_{yy(adj)}$, $E_{yy(adj)}$ and $B_{yy(adj)}$, respectively), are computed as follows:

$$T_{yy(adj)} = T_{yy} - T_{xy}^2/T_{xx} = 5366.92 - (4153.75)^2/7784.25 = 3150.44,$$

$$E_{yy(adj)} = E_{yy} - E_{xy}^2/E_{xx} = 3670.75 - (4005.67)^2/5494.75 = 748.68,$$

$$B_{yy(adj)} = T_{yy(adj)} - E_{yy(adj)} = 3150.44 - 748.68 = 2401.76.$$

The F-ratio is then computed:

$$F = [B_{yy(adj)}/(k-1)]/[E_{yy(adj)}/(N-k-1)]$$

$$= [2401.76/(3-1)]/[748.68/(12-3-1)]$$

$$= 12.83.$$

This F-ratio is significant at the $\alpha = .05$ level ($F_{.05;2,8} = 4.46$), and the null hypothesis is rejected. This implies that the type of licensing does have differential effect, the exact nature of which has yet to be examined. The results of the above computations are summarized in Table 3.

Before initiating a detailed analysis of the exact nature of the group effects, it is appropriate to test the assumptions that have been made

TABLE 3

Analysis of Covariance for Completely Randomized Design with Data From Illustrative Example

Source of Variation	Sum of Squares and Cross Products			Adjusted Sum of Squares	Degrees of Freedom	Adjusted Mean Square	F-ratio
	XX	XY	YY				
Treatment	---	---	---	2401.76	2	1200.88	12.83
Error	5494.75	4005.67	3670.45	748.68	8	93.59	
Total	7784.25	4153.75	5366.92	3150.44	10		

[36]

concerning the covariance model. The first assumption to be tested is the equality of the within group regression coefficients. The covariance model assumes homogeneity of the within class regression. Therefore, if the null hypothesis of no difference in regression coefficients is rejected, the covariance model is inappropriate. This test (equation 14 requires the computation of the within group sum of squares for the cross product of X and Y for each group:

$$E_{xy_1} = \sum_{j=1}^{4} (X_{1j} - \bar{X}_1)(Y_{1j} - \bar{Y}_1)$$

$$= (190 - 215.50)(177 - 186.25) + \ldots$$
$$+ (217 - 215.50)(176 - 186.25)$$
$$= 2397.50$$

$$E_{xy_2} = \sum_{j=1}^{4} (X_{2j} - \bar{X}_2)(Y_{2j} - \bar{Y}_2)$$

$$= (252 - 241.50)(226 - 206.50) + \ldots$$
$$+ (246 - 241.50)(206 - 206.50)$$
$$= 357.00,$$

$$E_{xy_3} = \sum_{j=1}^{4} (X_{3j} - \bar{X}_3)(Y_{3j} - \bar{Y}_3)$$

$$= (206 - 209.75)(266 - 214.50) + \ldots$$
$$+ (177 - 209.75)(188 - 214.50)$$
$$= 1252.50,$$

and the within group sum of squares of X for each group:

$$E_{xx_1} = \sum_{j=1}^{4} (X_{1j} - \bar{X}_1)^2$$

$$= (190 - 215.50)^2 + \ldots + (217 - 215.50)^2$$

$$= 3185.00,$$

$$E_{xx_2} = \sum_{j=1}^{4}(X_{2j} - \bar{X}_2)^2$$

$$= (252 - 241.50)^2 + \ldots + (246 - 241.50)^2$$

$$= 315.00,$$

$$E_{xx_3} = \sum_{j=1}^{4}(X_{3j} - \bar{X}_3)^2$$

$$= (206 - 209.75)^2 + \ldots + (177 - 209.75)^2$$

$$= 1994.75.$$

With these values, the within class regression coefficients for each group are calculated:

$$b_{w_1} = E_{xy_1}/E_{xx_1} = 2397.50/3185.00 = 0.7527,$$

$$b_{w_2} = E_{xy_2}/E_{xx_2} = 357.00/315.00 = 1.1333,$$

$$b_{w_3} = E_{xy_3}/E_{xx_3} = 1252.50/1994.75 = 0.6279.$$

Given these terms, S_1 (equation 15) is computed:

$$S_1 = E_{yy} - \sum_{i=1}^{k} b_{w_i}^2 E_{xx_i}$$

$$= 3670.75 - (.7527^2 \times 3185.00 + 1.1333^2 \times 315.00 + .6278^2 \times 1994.75)$$

$$= 674.996.$$

And finally, the F-ratio is computed:

$$F = [(E_{yy(adj)} - S_1)/(k-1)]/[S_1/(N-2k)]$$

$$= [(748.680 - 674.996)/(3-1)]/[674.996/(12-6)]$$

$$= .3275$$

Given this F-value, there is no reason to reject the hypothesis of homogeneity of regression (at $\alpha = .10$, $F_{2,6} = 3.46$). Therefore, the observed data appear to be consistent with the assumption of a common coefficient for the covariate.

The second assumption to be tested is that the regression coefficient is nonzero. The covariance model assumes that the covariate is associated with the dependent variable and, therefore, its coefficient is nonzero. The test of the null hypothesis (equation 17) is given by:

$$F = E_{xy}^2 (N-k-1)/(E_{yy}E_{xx} - E_{xy}^2)$$

$$= (4007)^2 (12-3-1)/[(3670.75)(5494.75) - (4007)^2]$$

$$= 31.2237.$$

Given this F-value, the hypothesis that $\beta = 0$ is rejected (at $\alpha = .05$, $F_{1,8} = 5.32$) and the hypothesized model is consistent with the observed data.

To assist in the interpretation of the results, the adjusted group means are calculated (equation 13). These computations require the pooled within class regression coefficient:

$$b_w = E_{xy}/E_{xx} = 4005.67/5494.75 = 0.729.$$

The adjusted group mean for the control group (group 1) is:

$$\bar{Y}_{1(adj)} = \bar{Y}_1 - b_w(\bar{X}_1 - \bar{X}) = 186.25 - .729(215.50 - 222.25)$$

$$= 191.17.$$

For the group where only the package store was established (group 2), the adjusted mean is:

$$\bar{Y}_{2(adj)} = \bar{Y}_2 - b_w(\bar{X}_2 - \bar{X}) = 206.50 - .729(241.50 - 222.25)$$

$$= 192.46.$$

And for the group with both the package store and the licensed restaurant (group 3), the adjusted mean is:

$$\bar{Y}_{3(adj)} = \bar{Y}_3 - b_w(\bar{X}_3 - \bar{X}) = 214.50 - .729(209.75 - 222.25)$$

$$= 223.62.$$

In this study, the researchers were mostly interested in comparing group 3 (both package store and licensed restaurant) with the control group (group 1). Group 2 (package store only) was included in the study for exploratory reasons, since it was considered a possible alternative if it turned out not to be feasible to establish both the package store and the licensed restaurant. The a priori comparison of group 1 with group 3 is tested with the t-statistic (equation 19),

$$t = \sum_{i=1}^{3} c_i \bar{Y}_{i(adj)} \Bigg/ \sqrt{MSE_{(adj)}\left[\sum_{i=1}^{3} c_i^2/n_i + \left[\sum_{i=1}^{3} c_i(\bar{X}_i - \bar{X})\right]^2 \Big/ E_{xx}\right]}$$

$$= \frac{(+1)(191.17) + (0)(192.46) + (-1)(223.62)}{\sqrt{93.59\left[\dfrac{1}{4} + \dfrac{1}{4} + \dfrac{[(1)(215.50-222.25) + (-1)(209.75-222.25)]^2}{5494.75}\right]}}$$

$$= -4.7155$$

Given this calculated t-value, the null hypothesis, that the value of the contrast is zero, is rejected ($t_{.05;8}$ = 2.306). Consequently it is concluded that the mean accident rate was higher in group 3 than in the control group.

If the researchers, after obtaining a significant overall F-ratio, wanted to compare all means to each other, Tukey's test for a posteriori, non-orthogonal comparisons is appropriate. The first comparison between the control group (group 1) and group 3 (both package store and licensed restaurant) is given by (equation 20):

$$q = [c_1 \bar{Y}_{1(adj)} + c_3 \bar{Y}_{3(adj)}] \Bigg/ \sqrt{\frac{MSE_{(adj)}}{n}\left[1 + \frac{B_{xx}/(k-1)}{E_{xx}}\right]}$$

$$= \frac{(+1)(191.17) + (-1)(223.62)}{\sqrt{\dfrac{93.585}{4}\left[1 + \dfrac{2289.5/2}{5494.75}\right]}}$$

$$= -6.103.$$

Given this calculated q-value the null hypothesis, that the two group means are equal, is rejected at the $\alpha = .05$ level ($q_{8,3} = 4.04$). The researchers would conclude that group 3 has higher mean accident rate than the control group. The second comparison between the control group and group 2 (package-store only) is given by:

$$q = [c_1 \bar{Y}_{1(adj)} + c_2 \bar{Y}_{2(adj)}] \Bigg/ \sqrt{\frac{MSE_{(adj)}}{n} \left[1 + \frac{B_{xx}/(k-1)}{E_{xx}} \right]}$$

$$= \frac{(+1)(191.17) + (-1)(192.46)}{5.317}$$

$$= -.243.$$

This difference is not significant ($q_{.05,8,3} = 4.04$) and the researchers would conclude that no difference exists between these two groups. The third comparison between groups 2 and 3 is given by:

$$q = [c_2 \bar{Y}_{2(adj)} + c_3 \bar{Y}_{3(adj)}] \Bigg/ \sqrt{\frac{MSE_{(adj)}}{n} \left[1 + \frac{B_{xx}/(k-1)}{E_{xx}} \right]}$$

$$= \frac{(+1)(192.46) + (-1)(223.62)}{5.317}$$

$$= -5.860$$

For this calculated q-value the null hypothesis is rejected and the researchers would conclude that group 3 (package store and licensed restaurant) has a higher mean accident rate than group 2 (package store only).

GEOMETRIC REPRESENTATION

In order to make it easier for those who are not mathematically oriented to see what is done in analysis of covariance, a graphical representation of the numeric example is provided.

In Figure 1, the data for the three groups, with four observations in each group, are shown. The horizontal axis gives the values of the covariate, traffic accident rate during the previous year, and the vertical axis gives

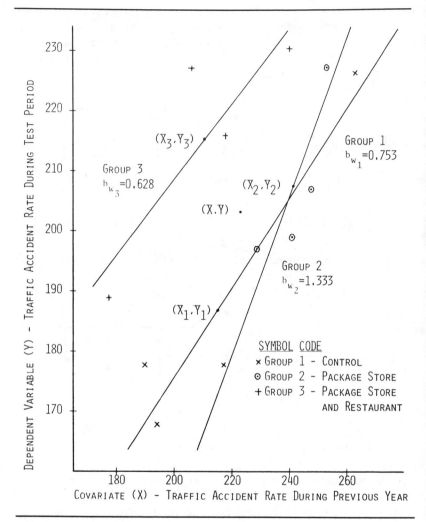

Figure 1: Within Class Regression Lines (Unique Slopes)

the values of the dependent variable, traffic accident rate in the test year. Also, regression lines computed separately for each group are indicated. As can be seen in Figure 1, the separate regression lines have slopes which are fairly close (parallel) to each other. In the previous section the test statistic for the homogeneity of these regression slopes was calculated, and it was found that the null hypothesis of homogeneity of regression could not be rejected.

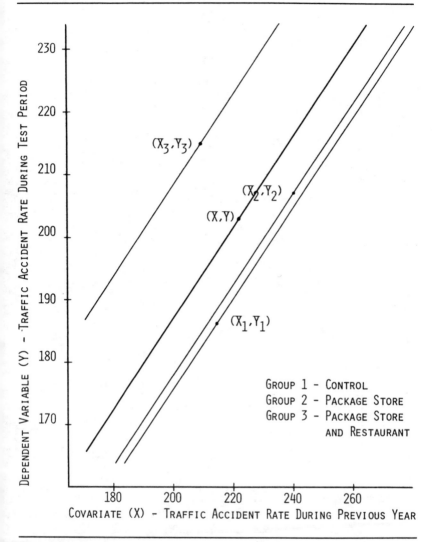

Figure 2: **Lines of Common Slope (bw = 0.729) Through Group Centroids**

In Figure 2, lines with common slope are drawn through each group centroid $(\overline{X}_i, \overline{Y}_i)$ and through the centroid of all observations $(\overline{X}, \overline{Y})$. The slope ($b_w = .729$) of these lines is derived by pooling all observations and adjusting for mean differences among groups. (One would get this regression slope by superimposing the group centroids on top of each other, i.e., adjusting so that all groups have the same mean value for both

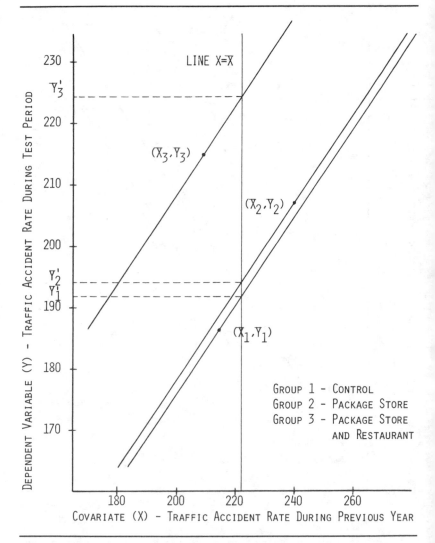

Figure 3: Graphical Representation of Adjusted Group Means

X and Y, and conducting a regular regression analysis.) Group effects are represented by the vertical differences (measured on the Y axis) between the lines going through group centroids and the line going through the centroid of all observations.

The adjusted group means, $\overline{Y}_i'$, are shown in Figure 3. The adjusted means are obtained from the intersection of the within group regression lines (with common slope) and the line, $X = \overline{X}$. Thus, a group mean is adjusted by moving it along the line which passes thorugh the group centroid and has slope b_w so that its value on the X axis is equal to the sample mean, $\overline{X}$. The adjusted treatment means are read from the Y axis. From Figure 3, it can be seen that groups 1 and 2 (control group and package store only, respectively) have considerably different unadjusted group means, but when adjusted for the value of the covariate the means of these two groups are very close to each other. Also, it is observed that for group 3 (both package store and licensed restaurant) the adjusted mean is much higher than for the two other groups. (The regression line going through group 3 centroid is considerable above the other two lines, i.e., it has a considerably higher intercept).

ALTERNATE PERSPECTIVE OF TESTING WITH ANALYSIS OF COVARIANCE

In the preceding discussion, mention has been made of a number of statistical tests, e.g., test for homogeneity of regression coefficients and test for absence of group or treatment effects. It is often helpful to view these tests as a comparison of alternate models. Figure 4 presents five alternate statistical models within the context of a completely randomized design. Model 1 considers the observed value of the dependent variable to be a function of two components: the overall mean and an error term. Model 2, the usual analysis of variance model for the completely ran-domized design, considers the observed valued of the dependent variable to be a function of three components: the overall mean, the group or treatment effect and an error term. With the analysis of variance model, testing that all group effects are identically zero is equivalent to comparing Model 1 to Model 2. If Model 1 explains the variability of the dependent variable as well as Model 2, it can be concluded that the inclusion of the group effect component contributes nothing to the explanatory power of Model 2, and the null hypothesis that all group effects are identically zero may not be rejected.

Let SS_1 be the variation (sum of squares) in the dependent variable explained by the explanatory terms (excluding the error term) in Model 1, and SS_2 be the variation explained by the explanatory terms in Model 2. The difference, $SS_2 - SS_1$, is the "extra sum of squares" due to the in-clusion of the extra terms (τ_i's) in Model 2. Since the total sum of squares, T_{yy}, is the same in both models, the difference in the explained variation may be expressed as the difference in the unexplained, or error, variation. Therefore, the extra sum of squares is equal to $E_{yy1} - E_{yy2}$,

MODEL 1: $Y_{ij} = u + e_{ij}$

MODEL 2: $Y_{ij} = u + \tau_i + e_{ij}$

MODEL 3: $Y_{ij} = u + \beta(X_{ij} - \bar{X}) + e_{ij}$

MODEL 4: $Y_{ij} = u + \tau_i + \beta(X_{ij} - \bar{X}) + e_{ij}$

MODEL 5: $Y_{ij} = u + \tau_i + \beta_i(X_{ij} - \bar{X}) + e_{ij}$

Y_{ij}	=	OBSERVED VALUE OF THE DEPENDENT VARIABLE
u	=	OVERALL MEAN
τ_i	=	EFFECT DUE TO iTH LEVEL OF CATEGORICAL INDEPENDENT VARIABLE
β_i	=	COEFFICIENT OF COVARIATE FOR GROUP i
β	=	COEFFICIENT OF COVARIATE, COMMON FOR ALL GROUPS
X_{ij}	=	OBSERVED VALUE OF THE COVARIATE
$\bar{X}$	=	MEAN OF THE COVARIATE
e_{ij}	=	RANDOM ERROR

Figure 4: Alternate Statistical Models Under Completely Randomized Design

where E_{yyk} is the error sum of squares of Y for Model k. The degrees of freedom associated with this extra sum of squares is equal to the difference in the degrees of freedom of the component parts, or $(N-1) - (N-k) = k-1$. *If* all group effects are identically zero, this difference (extra sum of squares) will be due strictly to sampling error, and it can be shown that the expected value of $(E_{yy1} - E_{yy2})/ (k-1)$ is equal to $\sigma_{\mathcal{E}}^2$, the variance of the error term. Irrespective of the existence of group effects the expected value of $E^{yy2}/N-k$ is equal to $\sigma_{\mathcal{E}}^2$. With the added assumption that the errors are normally distributed, the ratio

$$F = \frac{(E_{yy1} - E_{yy2})/(k-1)}{E_{yy2}/(N-k)} \qquad [22]$$

is distributed as the F-distribution, with k-1 and N-k degree of freedom, under the null hypothesis of no group effects. This F-ratio provides a

ROCKHURST COLLEGE LIBRARY

means to statistically test the significance of the "extra" terms included in Model 2.

This same extra sum of squares principle may be applied to the analysis of covariance model. In the discussion to follow, three hypotheses are considered:

(1) homogeneity of regression coefficients,
(2) zero value of β, and
(3) absence of group or treatment effects.

Testing the homogeneity of regression coefficients is equivalent to comparing Model 4, with a common value of β over all groups or treatment levels, to Model 5, having unique values of β for each group. Under the null hypothesis of homogeneity, the extra sum of squares explained by the inclusion of separate β values should not be statistically significant. The test used here is similar to that mentioned above, and considers the ratio,

$$F = \frac{(E_{yy4} - E_{yy5})/[(N-k-1) - (N-2k)]}{E_{yy5}/(N-2k)} \qquad [23]$$

which under the null hypothesis, $H_0: \beta_1 = \beta_2 = \ldots \beta_k = \beta$, is distributed as the F-distribution with k-1 and N-2k degrees of freedom. It is noted that

$$E_{yy4} = E_{yy(adj)} = E_{yy} - b_w^2 E_{xx}$$

(recall equation 10), and

$$E_{yy5} = E_{yy} - \Sigma b_{w_i}^2 E_{xx_i}.$$

Therefore, equation 23 may be restated as,

$$F = \frac{[(E_{yy} - b_w^2 E_{xx}) - (E_{yy} - \Sigma b_{w_i}^2 E_{xx_i})]/[(N-k-1) - (N-2k)]}{(E_{yy} - \Sigma b_{w_i}^2 E_{xx_i})/(N-2k)}$$

$$= \frac{(\Sigma b_{w_i}^2 E_{xx_i} - b_w^2 E_{xx})/(k-1)}{(E_{yy} - \Sigma b_{w_i}^2 E_{xx_i})/(N-2k)}. \qquad [24]$$

132238

The reader will note that this is the same F-ratio (see equation 16) presented in an earlier section for testing this same hypothesis.

Likewise, testing the hypothesis, H_0: $\beta = 0$, under the assumption of homogeneity of regression coefficients is equivalent to comparing Model 2 to Model 4. The appropriate F-ratio for this test is,

$$F = \frac{(E_{yy2} - E_{yy4})/[(N-k) - (N-k-1)]}{E_{yy4}/(N-k-1)} \qquad [25]$$

which under the null hypothesis is distributed as the F-distribution with 1 and $N-k-1$ degrees of freedom. Since $E_{yy2} = E_{yy}$, equation 25 may be restated as,

$$F = \frac{(E_{yy} - E_{yy(adj)})/[(N-k) - (N-k-1)]}{E_{yy(adj)}/(N-k-1)}$$

$$= \frac{b_w^2 E_{xx}}{(E_{yy} - b_w^2 E_{xx})/(N-k-1)}$$

$$= \frac{E_{xy}^2}{(E_{yy}E_{xx} - E_{xy}^2)/(N-k-1)} . \qquad [26]$$

The reader will note that equation 26 is identical to the previously mentioned F-ratio for testing this hypothesis given in equation 17.

Lastly, testing the hypothesis that all group effects are identically zero under the assumption of homogeneous regression coefficients is equivalent to comparing Model 3 to Model 4. The appropriate F-ratio for this test is

$$F = \frac{(E_{yy3} - E_{yy4})/[(N-2) - (N-k-1)]}{E_{yy4}/(N-k-1)} \qquad [27]$$

which under the null hypothesis, H_0: $\tau_i = 0$ for all i, is distributed as the F-distribution with $k-1$ and $N-k-1$ degrees of freedom. But from the development of equation 5, it is noted that $E_{yy3} = T_{yy(adj)}$. Therefore, equation 27 may be restated as,

$$= \frac{[T_{yy(adj)} - E_{yy(adj)}]/[(N-2) - (N-k-1)]}{E_{yy(adj)}/(N-k-1)}$$

$$= \frac{B_{yy(adj)}/(k-1)}{E_{yy(adj)}/(N-k-1)} \qquad [28]$$

which is equivalent to the overall F-test in the completely randomized analysis of covariance model (equation 12).

Other Problem Perspectives

Earlier, it was mentioned that analysis of covariance could be utilized under three alternate problem perspectives. From the viewpoint of the statistical model all three perspectives are quite similar. But, in conducting the analysis, the method of partitioning the sum of squares is different. Statistical testing, within the context of analysis of covariance, is accomplished through mean square comparisons, where the mean squares are computed by dividing sums of squares by the appropriate degrees of freedom. The problem perspective taken by the researcher will influence the method of partitioning the total sum of squares into its various components and, therefore, may affect the outcome of the statistical testing.

In all cases, the total sum of squares, not adjusted for the covariate (i.e., sum of squared deviations of the dependent variable from its mean) is partitioned into the sum of squares explained collectively by the independent variables (including the covariate) and the sum of squares error. Since the error term is assumed independent of the explanatory variables, the sum of squares error plus sum of squares explained will always add to equal the total sum of squares. The explained sum of squares must then be partitioned into components associated with each of the independent variables. The method employed in this partitioning is conditional upon the analysis perspective taken.

With the experimental perspective, which has been extensively considered up to this point, the sum of squares explained by the covariate is computed without giving consideration to the categorical independent variable. The sum of squares associated with the categorical independent variable is then computed by subtracting the sum of squares explained by the covariate from the sum of squares explained by the independent variables collectively. This is a hierarchical, or sequential, procedure whereby the sum of squares assigned to the categorical independent variable is the residual of the explained sum of squares left after the covariance adjustment is taken.

With the second perspective the adjustment is first made for the categorical independent variable rather than the covariate. The sum of squares associated with the categorical independent variable is computed first, and the sum of squares associated with the covariate is the residual which is left after subtracting the sum of squares due to the categorical independent variable from the sum of squares explained by the independent variables collectively. That is, the sum of squares attributable to the covariate represents the explained variation remaining after removing the effects of the categorical independent variable. This is also a hierarchical, or sequential, procedure but the order in which the variables are treated is opposite of that of the experimental perspective.

With the third, or regression perspective, both variables are of equal interest and a nonhierarchical procedure, sometimes referred to as a "partial" procedure, is used. The sum of squares for the covariate is the explained variation attributable to the covariate after the adjustment is made for the categorical independent variable, and the sum of squares attributable to the categorical independent variable is that portion of the explained variation after adjustment has been made for the covariate. (With the regression perspective, the sum of squares of the covariate and the categorical independent variable need not necessarily add up to the total explained sum of squares.)

The degree to which the sum of squares in each of these analyses will differ is a function of the relationship between the covariate and the other independent variable. Ideally, the mean value of the covariate will be equal over all levels of the categorical independent variable, in which case all three analyses will yield the same results. However, since direct control is usually not imposed, the mean value of the covariate over the various levels of the categorical independent variable is not likely to be identical. (This is particularly true for observational and experimental studies where intact groups are employed.) This will result in some degree of correlation, or overlap in the explanatory power of covariate and the categorical independent variable. Therefore, depending upon the nature of the relationship, the computed mean squares and associated F-ratios may well vary depending upon the approach employed in the particular analysis. Analysis procedures under the second and regression perspectives are now considered.

ANALYSIS UNDER SECOND PERSPECTIVE

Under the second perspective, which is usually taken only in observational studies, interest centers on the relationship between the covariate and the dependent variable within distinct categorically defined groups. We call this design a "regression within groups design." In this design one tries to "partial out" the effect of the categorical variable from the error term and, hence, get more precise information on the relationship of the covariate with the dependent variable. The focus in this analysis is testing for significant within group correlation between the covariate and the dependent variable, and estimating the nature of this relationship while controlling for the differences among group means. This kind of design is only employed in observational studies, and the same warnings are applicable here as those given earlier in connection with observational studies.

The statistical model under the regression within groups design is the same as that under the completely randomized design and the computational procedures differ only slightly. As under all three perspectives, the computation of the total sum of squares of Y (adjusted only for the grand mean), T_{yy}, and the adjusted error sum of squares of Y, $E_{yy(adj)}$, remain unchanged. Under the regression within groups design the categorical independent variable is the nuisance variable, and the adjusted (for groups) total sum of squares of Y, $T_{yy(adj)}$ is obtained by subtracting the (unadjusted) between groups sum of squares of Y, $B_{yy} = \Sigma n(\overline{Y}_i - \overline{Y})^2$, from the total sum of squares of Y as follows:

$$T_{yy(adj)} = T_{yy} - \sum_{i=1}^{k} n (\overline{Y}_i - \overline{Y})^2; \qquad [29]$$

and the adjusted (for groups) covariate sum of squares, $C_{yy(adj)}$ is computed:

$$C_{yy(adj)} = T_{yy(adj)} - E_{yy(adj)}. \qquad [30]$$

The degrees of freedom for $C_{yy(adj)}$ is equal to the number of covariates.

The statistical test for the null hypothesis of no covariate effects (i.e., $H_o: \beta = 0$) is given by:

$$F = \frac{C_{yy(adj)}/1}{E_{yy(adj)}/(N-k-1)}. \qquad [31]$$

Under the null hypothesis this ratio has an F-distribution with 1 and $(N-k-1)$ degrees of freedom.

Under this perspective, as with the others, the test of homogeneity of regression is given by equation 14 and b_w, given by equation 8, is an unbiased estimator of β. Also, a test for significant group effects can be made by using the ratio:

$$F = \frac{B_{yy}/(k-1)}{E_{yy(adj)}/(N-k-1)} \, , \qquad [32]$$

which under the null hypothesis of no group effects has an F-distribution with $k-1$ and $N-k-1$ degrees of freedom.

The analysis of covariance table for the regression within group design is presented in Table 4.

ANALYSIS UNDER REGRESSION PERSPECTIVE

Under the regression perspective, the covariate and categorical independent variable are of equal interest. The analysis under this problem perspective is identical to the least-squares regression analysis. The total sum of squares of Y (adjusted only for the grand mean), T_{yy}, and the adjusted error sum of squares of Y, $E_{yy(adj)}$, are computed as before. The between group (treatment) sum of squares of Y adjusted for the covariate is:

$$B_{yy(adj \, for \, Co)} = T_{yy(adj \, for \, Co)} - E_{yy(adj)}, \qquad [33]$$

where

$$T_{yy(adj \, for \, Co)} = T_{yy} - T_{xy}^2/T_{xx}. \qquad [34]$$

And the covariate sum of squares of Y adjusted for the group effect is:

$$C_{yy(adj \, for \, Group)} = T_{yy(adj \, for \, Group)} = E_{yy(adj)}, \qquad [35]$$

where

$$T_{yy(adj \, for \, Group)} = T_{yy} - \sum_{i=1}^{k} n \, (Y_i - Y)^2. \qquad [36]$$

In this case there are two null hypotheses of interest; the first is that the group effect is zero (H_o: $\tau_i = 0$, for all i), and the second is that the covariate

TABLE 4
Analysis of Covariance for Regression Within Groups Design

SOURCE OF VARIATION	SUM OF SQUARES AND CROSS PRODUCTS			ADJUSTED SUM OF SQUARES	DEGREES OF FREEDOM	ADJUSTED MEAN SQUARE	F-RATIO
	XX	XY	YY				
COVARIATE	--	--	--	$C_{YY(ADJ)}$	1	$\dfrac{C_{YY(ADJ)}}{}$	$\dfrac{MSC(ADJ)}{MSE(ADJ)}$
ERROR	E_{XX}	E_{XY}	E_{YY}	$E_{YY(ADJ)}$	N-K-1	$\dfrac{E_{YY(ADJ)}}{N-K-1}$	
TOTAL	--	--	T_{YY}	$T_{YY(ADJ)}$	N-K		

$E_{xx} = \Sigma\Sigma(X_{ij} - \bar{X}_i)^2$

$E_{xy} = \Sigma\Sigma(X_{ij} - \bar{X}_i)(Y_{ij} - \bar{Y}_i)$

$E_{yy} = \Sigma\Sigma(Y_{ij} - \bar{Y}_i)^2$

$T_{yy} = \Sigma\Sigma(Y_{ij} - \bar{Y})^2$

$E_{yy(adj)} = E_{yy} - E_{xy}^2/E_{xx}$

$T_{yy(adj)} = T_{yy} - \Sigma n(\bar{Y}_i - \bar{Y})^2$

$C_{yy(adj)} = T_{yy(adj)} - E_{yy(adj)}$

$b_w = E_{xy}/E_{xx}$

[53]

effect is zero (H_o: $\beta = 0$). The statistical test for group effect is given by:

$$F = \frac{B_{yy(\text{adj for Co})}/(k-1)}{E_{yy(\text{adj})}/(N-k-1)} , \qquad [37]$$

which, under the null hypothesis, has an F-distribution with $k-1$ and $N-k-1$ degrees of freedom. The test for covariate effect is given by:

$$F = \frac{C_{yy(\text{adj for Group})}/1}{E_{yy(\text{adj})}/(N-k-1)} , \qquad [38]$$

which, under the null hypothesis, has an F-distribution with 1 and $N-k-1$ degrees of freedom. The test for homogeneity of regression is unchanged and is given by equation 14; and b_w, given by equation 8, is an unbiased estimator of β.

The analysis of covariance table for the regression perspective is given in Table 5.

5. ANALYSIS OF COVARIANCE FOR MORE COMPLEX LAYOUTS

The preceding section considers only the one-way layout which is characterized by a single categorical independent variable with k levels and the covariate. In many situations, both observational and experimental, one may wish to consider two or more categorical independent variables. Situations such as these, which also involve quantitative independent variables (covariates), may be analyzed using an analysis of covariance model.

In considering two or more categorical independent variables in conjunction with covariates, a large number of model configurations are possible. However, the analysis procedures used for these models are in part influenced by the distribution of observations over the levels of the categorical independent variables. The analysis for the one-way layout generally is unaffected by the uneven distribution of observations over groups—unequal group or cell size. (The only modification needed to the analysis procedures already presented to handle unequal cell sizes is to replace n by n_i and define $N = \Sigma n_i$.) However, when two or more categorical independent variables are considered matters become more complicated.

TABLE 5
Analysis of Covariance for Regression Design

Source of Variation	Adjusted Sum of Squares	Degrees of Freedom	Adjusted Mean Square	F-Ratio
Treatment	$B_{YY\text{(ADJ FOR COV)}}$	$K-1$	$\dfrac{B_{YY\text{(ADJ FOR COV)}}}{K-1}$	$\dfrac{MST_{\text{(ADJ)}}}{MSE_{\text{(ADJ)}}}$
Covariate	$C_{YY\text{(ADJ FOR GROUP)}}$	1	$\dfrac{C_{YY\text{(ADJ FOR GROUP)}}}{1}$	$\dfrac{MSC_{\text{(ADJ)}}}{MSE_{\text{(ADJ)}}}$
Error	$E_{YY\text{(ADJ)}}$	$N-K-1$	$\dfrac{E_{YY\text{(ADJ)}}}{N-K-1}$	
Total	T_{YY}	$N-1$		

$B_{yy} = \Sigma n(\overline{Y}_i - \overline{Y})^2$

$E_{xx} = \Sigma\Sigma(X_{ij} - \overline{X}_i)^2$

$E_{xy} = \Sigma\Sigma(X_{ij} - \overline{X}_i)(Y_{ij} - \overline{Y}_i)$

$E_{yy} = \Sigma\Sigma(Y_{ij} - \overline{Y}_i)^2$

$T_{yy} = \Sigma\Sigma(Y_{ij} - \overline{Y})^2$

$E_{yy(adj)} = E_{yy} - E_{xy}^2/E_{xx}$

$T_{yy(adj \text{ for } Cov)} = T_{yy} - T_{xy}^2/T_{xy}$

$T_{yy(adj \text{ for } Group)} = T_{yy} - B_{yy}$

$B_{yy(adj \text{ for } Cov)} = T_{yy(adj \text{ for } Cov)} - E_{yy(adj)}$

$C_{yy(adj \text{ for } Group)} = T_{yy(adj \text{ for } Group)} - E_{yy(adj)}$

$b_w = E_{xy}/E_{xx}$

With more than one categorical independent variable, the ideal situation is to have what is referred to as "balanced" observations, that is, observations that occur with equal or proportional frequency in each level of every categorical independent variable. For such balanced designs available statistical procedures allow the analyst to partition the sum of squares associated with a particular categorical independent variable, so that it is independent of the sums of squares associated with each other categorical independent variable. However, if observations are not balanced, it becomes impossible to assign the sum of squares to a single categorical independent variable in such a way that it is not influenced by the other categorical independent variables.

The analysis procedures considered in this section are generally applicable to balanced designs. In cases where the data are not balanced, it is recommended that the effect or contribution of one categorical independent variable be measured in terms of its "partial" or marginal sum of squares. The partial sum of squares represents the sum of squares explained by the given variable after the impact of the other independent variables have been accounted for. The statistical procedure employed in these cases is the method of least squares (regression analysis with dummy variables).

The preceding discussion deals only with categorical independent variables. If in addition to categorical independent variables, the model has a covariate, the covariate may still be handled in any of three ways, as previously discussed (pages 49-54) under the three alternate problem perspectives. However, with unbalanced designs, since the categorical independent variables are analyzed using the least squares method, it is most often the case that the regression perspective is taken and all independent variables (categorical and covariates) are analyzed using least squares.

In observational studies the researcher has no direct control over the test units and, consequently, has no influence on the distribution of observations over the levels of the categorical independent variables. In other words, the researcher has no way to insure that each level of a given categorical independent variable has an equal (or proportional) number of observations, on each level of every other categorical independent variable. If the data from an observational study are such that they are balanced, then the analysis procedures discussed in this section are appropriate. But if the data are not balanced it is recommended that the data be analyzed using regression analysis with dummy variables.

In experimental settings the researcher can exert direct or experimental control over the assignment of treatments (categorical independent variables), and is able to achieve a balanced or near balanced design.

For cases such as these a number of designs and associated analysis procedures have been developed. In the remainder of this section a number of procedures for analysis of covariance with two or more categorical independent variables are discussed. These procedures are most commonly employed in the context of experimental studies and will be discussed accordingly.

Randomized Complete Block Design

In some experimental settings interest centers on a single categorical independent variable as in the one-way layout, but the researcher is able to identify one or more characteristics of the test units which will influence the value of the dependent variable. In such cases, it is sometimes possible to group similar test units (test units are grouped so that the variability of test units within any grouping, referred to as a block, is less than the variability among the groupings). This results in an experiment with two categorical independent variables: the initial variable of interst, and a second variable representing the groupings (blocks) of test units included in an effort to increase the precision of the experiment. If this second variable were not included, the design would be a completely randomized design and the variation in the dependent variable attributable to this second variable would be included in the error term. But by including the second variable, a portion of the error variance is accounted for by this variable (representing test unit characteristics). Therefore, the error variance is reduced, enabling the researcher to increase the accuracy of the experiment. Given this perspective, it is seen that blocking is a form of direct control which reduces experimental error by controlling variability due to the heterogeneity of test units.

Designs such as the one described above are called randomized block designs. When such designs include a quantitative independent variable in addition to the two categorical independent variables, they are analyzed using a randomized block analysis of covariance model.

An additional condition for the use of the randomized block design is that the treatment levels can be randomly assigned to the test units within each block. An exception is made to the randomization procedure when a block consists of one test unit which receives all treatment levels. In this case, the order of treatment levels is randomly determined for each test unit, given that the nature of the experiment allows this. The randomized block design is not applied to observational data.

While there are a number of different ways of blocking, the discussion to follow considers only the randomized complete block design with one observation per cell, i.e., every treatment level is assigned to one test unit from each block. Therefore, each block contains k (the number of treatment levels) test units and there are n blocks, where n is the number of replications desired for the experiment. (For an example of the randomized complete block analysis of covariance design refer to page 64.)

COVARIANCE MODEL

The linear model for the randomized complete block analysis of covariance with one covariate is,

$$Y_{ij} = u + \tau_i + R_j + \beta(X_{ij} - \bar{X}) + e_{ij}; \qquad [39]$$

$$i=1, \ldots, k; \quad j=1, \ldots, n;$$

where Y_{ij} is the observed value of the dependent variable for the i*th* treatment level and the j*th* block, u is the true mean effect, τ_i is the effect due to the i*th* level of the categorical independent variable (treatment) where $\Sigma\tau_i = 0$, R_j is the effect due to the j*th* block where $\Sigma R_j = 0$, β is the (regression) coefficient of the covariate, X_{ij} is the observed value of the covariate, $\bar{X}$ is the general mean of the covariate, and e_{ij} is the random error which is normally and independently distributed with mean zero and variance σ^2.

For the randomized block design, primary interest lies in examining the differences among treatment effects, and both the blocking variable and the covariate(s) are nuisance variables which are included to increase the precision of the experiment. As in the completely randomized design, the hypothesis of no treatment effects is tested using an F-ratio of adjusted mean squares. To conduct this test it is necessary to compute the adjusted treatment sum of squares of Y, $B_{yy(adj)}$ and the adjusted error sum of squares of Y, $E_{yy(adj)}$.

The rationale and the development of the computational procedure for the adjusted error sum of squares of Y, $E_{yy(adj)}$, for the randomized complete block design are directly analogous to those of the completely randomized design and are not repeated here. The computational equation for $E_{yy(adj)}$ is;

$$E_{yy(adj)} = E_{yy} - b_w^2 E_{xx} = E_{yy} - E_{xy}^2/E_{xx} \qquad [40]$$

where,

$$E_{yy} = \sum_{i=1}^{k} \sum_{j=1}^{n} (Y_{ij} - \bar{Y}_{i\cdot} - \bar{Y}_{\cdot j} + \bar{Y})^2,$$

$$E_{xy} = \sum_{i=1}^{k} \sum_{j=1}^{n} (X_{ij} - \bar{X}_{i\cdot} - \bar{X}_{\cdot j} + \bar{X})(Y_{ij} - \bar{Y}_{i\cdot} - \bar{Y}_{\cdot j} + \bar{Y}),$$

$$E_{xx} = \sum_{i=1}^{k} \sum_{j=1}^{n} (X_{ij} - \bar{X}_{i\cdot} - \bar{X}_{\cdot j} + \bar{X})^2, \text{ and}$$

$$b_w = E_{xy}/E_{xx}$$

with $\bar{Y}_{i\cdot}$ equal to the mean of the Y_{ij} for treatment i, $\bar{Y}_{\cdot j}$ the mean value for block j and corresponding definitions on $\bar{X}_{i\cdot}$ and $\bar{X}_{\cdot j}$. The degrees of freedom for $E_{yy(adj)}$ are $(n-1)(k-1)-1$.

In the completely randomized design the adjusted between group (treatment) sum of squares, $B_{yy(adj)}$, is computed by subtracting the adjusted within group sum of squares, $E_{yy(adj)}$, from the adjusted total sum of squares, $T_{yy(adj)}$. Following this procedure with the randomized block design will yield an adjusted sum of squares, which includes block effects as well as treatment effects. Therefore, an alternate procedure, described in the following paragraph, is utilized to compute the adjusted treatment sum of squares.

Assume that all treatment effects are zero, i.e., $\tau_i = 0$ for all i, then the adjusted within group sum of squares of Y would be computed as in the one-way layout (equation 10) as:

$$E^*_{yy(adj)} = E^*_{yy} - E^{*2}_{xy}/E^*_{xx} \qquad [41]$$

where;

$$E^*_{yy} = \sum_{i=1}^{k} \sum_{j=1}^{n} (Y_{ij} - \bar{Y}_{\cdot j})^2,$$

$$E^*_{xy} = \sum_{i=1}^{k} \sum_{j=1}^{n} (X_{ij} - \bar{X}_{\cdot j})(Y_{ij} - \bar{Y}_{\cdot j}), \text{ and}$$

$$E^*_{xx} = \sum_{i=1}^{k} \sum_{j=1}^{n} (X_{ij} - \bar{X}_{\cdot j})^2.$$

If this assumption that all treatment effects are zero is not valid, then $E^*_{yy(adj)}$ consists of both treatment effects and error effects. But the adjusted error sum of squares, $E_{yy(adj)}$ has been calculated (equation 40), therefore, the adjusted treatment sum of squares of Y, $B_{yy(adj)}$, may be obtained by subtraction as follows:

$$B_{yy(adj)} = E^*_{yy(adj)} - E_{yy(adj)}. \qquad [42]$$

Further, it can be shown that

$$E^*_{yy} = B_{yy} + E_{yy},$$

$$E^*_{xy} = B_{xy} + E_{xy}, \text{ and}$$

$$E^*_{xx} = B_{xx} + E_{xx}$$

where,

$$B_{yy} = n \sum_{i=1}^{k} (\bar{Y}_{i\bullet} - \bar{Y})^2,$$

$$B_{xy} = n \sum_{i=1}^{k} (\bar{X}_{i\bullet} - \bar{X})(\bar{Y}_{i\bullet} - \bar{Y}), \text{ and}$$

$$B_{xx} = n \sum_{i=1}^{k} (\bar{X}_{i\bullet} - \bar{X})^2.$$

Therefore, equation 42 is expressed:

$$B_{yy(adj)} = (B_{yy} + E_{yy}) - (B_{xy} + E_{xy})^2/(B_{xx} + E_{xx}) - E_{yy(adj)}. \qquad [43]$$

The degrees of freedom for $B_{yy(adj)}$ are $(nk-n-1)-(n-1)(k-1)-1=k-1$, the difference in the degrees of freedom of the terms in equation 42.

With the computation of the adjusted treatment and error sums of squares, the hypothesis of no treatment effects can be tested. This statistical test amounts to testing the null hypothesis that $\tau_i = 0$ for all i. The test statistic is the F-ratio,

$$F = \frac{B_{yy(adj)}/(k-1)}{E_{yy(adj)}/(N-n-k)} \qquad [44]$$

which, under the null hypothesis, has an F-distribution with k-1 and N-n-k degrees of freedom.

If one is interested in testing for block effects, an adjusted block sum of squares of Y, designated $S_{yy(adj)}$, is computed by a procedure analogous to that used in computing $B_{yy(adj)}$. The computational form is:

$$S_{yy(adj)} = (S_{yy} + E_{yy}) - (S_{xy} + E_{xy})^2/(S_{xx} + E_{xx}) - E_{yy(adj)} \qquad [45]$$

where;

$$S_{yy} = k \sum_{j=1}^{n} (\bar{Y}_{\cdot j} - \bar{Y})^2,$$

$$S_{xy} = k \sum_{j=1}^{n} (\bar{X}_{\cdot j} - \bar{X})(\bar{Y}_{\cdot j} - \bar{Y}), \text{ and}$$

$$S_{xx} = k \sum_{j=1}^{n} (\bar{X}_{\cdot j} - \bar{X})^2.$$

The degrees of freedom for $S_{yy(adj)}$ are $(nk-k-1) - (n-1)(k-1) = n-1$. The F-ratio used to test the null hypothesis of no block effects, i.e., $R_j = 0$ for all j, is:

$$F = \frac{S_{yy(adj)}/(n-1)}{E_{yy(adj)}/(N-n-k)} \qquad [46]$$

which, under the null hypothesis, has an F-distribution with n-1 and N-n-k degrees of freedom.

The analysis of covariance table for the randomized block design is presented in Table 6.

TABLE 6
Analysis of Covariance for Randomized Complete Block Design

Source of Variation	Sum of Squares and Cross Products			Adjusted Sum of Squares	Degrees of Freedom	Adjusted Mean Square	Expected Mean Square	F-Ratio
	XX	XY	YY					
Block	S_{XX}	S_{XY}	S_{YY}	$S_{YY(ADJ)}$	$N-1$	$\dfrac{S_{YY(ADJ)}}{N-1}$	$\sigma^2_{\epsilon\mid\beta} + \dfrac{K\Sigma R_J^2}{N-1}$	$\dfrac{MSB_{(ADJ)}}{MSE_{(ADJ)}}$
Treatment	B_{XX}	B_{XY}	B_{YY}	$B_{YY(ADJ)}$	$K-1$	$\dfrac{B_{YY(ADJ)}}{K-1}$	$\sigma^2_{\epsilon\mid\beta} + \dfrac{N\Sigma\tau_I^2}{K-1}$	$\dfrac{MST_{(ADJ)}}{MSE_{(ADJ)}}$
Error	E_{XX}	E_{XY}	E_{YY}	$E_{YY(ADJ)}$	$(N-1)(K-1)-1$	$\dfrac{E_{YY(ADJ)}}{N-N-K}$	$\sigma^2_{\epsilon\mid\beta}$	
Total					$N-2$			

$S_{xx} = k\Sigma(\overline{X}_{.j} - \overline{X})^2$

$S_{xy} = k\Sigma(\overline{X}_{.j} - \overline{X})(\overline{Y}_{.j} - \overline{Y})$

$S_{yy} = k\Sigma(\overline{Y}_{.j} - \overline{Y})^2$

$B_{xx} = n\Sigma(\overline{X}_{i.} - \overline{X})^2$

$B_{xy} = n\Sigma(\overline{X}_{i.} - \overline{X})(\overline{Y}_{i.} - \overline{Y})$

$B_{yy} = n\Sigma(\overline{Y}_{i.} - \overline{Y})^2$

$E_{xx} = \Sigma\Sigma(X_{ij} - \overline{X}_{i.} - \overline{X}_{.j} + \overline{X})^2$

$E_{xy} = \Sigma\Sigma(X_{ij} - \overline{X}_{i.} - \overline{X}_{.j} + \overline{X})(Y_{ij} - \overline{Y}_{i.} - \overline{Y}_{.j} + \overline{Y})$

$E_{yy} = \Sigma\Sigma(Y_{ij} - \overline{Y}_{i.} - \overline{Y}_{.j} + \overline{Y})^2$

$E_{yy(adj)} = E_{yy} - E_{xy}^2/E_{xx}$

$S_{yy(adj)} = (S_{yy} + E_{yy}) - (S_{xy} + E_{xy})^2/(S_{xx} + E_{xx}) - E_{yy(adj)}$

$B_{yy(adj)} = (B_{yy} + E_{yy}) - (B_{xy} + E_{xy})^2/(B_{xx} + E_{xx}) - E_{yy(adj)}$

TESTING β

For the randomized complete block analysis of covariance certain assumptions are made concerning the regression coefficient, i.e., homogeneity of regression and a nonzero regression coefficient. The test of the hypothesis that $\beta=0$ is a straightforward extention of the procedure utilized with the completely randomized design and is given by,

$$F = E_{xy}^2(N-n-k)/(E_{yy}E_{xx} - E_{xy}^2) \qquad [47]$$

where the error sum of squares terms, E_{xx}, E_{xy} and E_{yy}, have previously been defined in relation to equation 40. Under the null hypothesis, this statistic is distributed as the F-distribution with 1 and $N-n-k$ degrees of freedom.

The test for homogeneity of regression is considerably more complex for the randomized complete block design. One would like to test the hypothesis that the regression coefficients are equal across all treatment-block combinations; but with only one observation per treatment-block combination it is impossible to conduct such a test. The most reasonable alternative is to test for homogeneity of regression across treatments under the assumptions of equal regression coefficients across blocks within treatments. In conducting this test, one would be tempted to proceed in a manner similar to that used with the completely randomized design (pages 27-28). The difficulty with this approach, i.e., using equation 14 with the error sum of squares consistent with the randomized block design, is that the computation of the error sum of squares for any single treatment uses all n block means and, therefore, utilizes information on observations from all other treatments. This results in b_w's and associated sums of squares which are not independent over treatments, and violates an assumption necessary for the F-test. The easiest solution to this dilemma is to test for homogeneity of regression coefficients using the "added sum of squares" principle as described in the section on "Alternative Perspective of Testing and with Analysis of Covariance" (see pages 45-49).

MEAN COMPARISONS

The adjusted treatment means for the randomized complete block analysis of covariance are computed in a manner identical to that used for the completely randomized design (see equation 13), with the exception that $b_w = E_{xy}/E_{xx}$ is computed using the error sums of squares and cross products computed for the randomized block design (see Table 6). Also, the comparisons among means for the randomized complete block analysis of covariance are identical to those of the completely randomized analysis of covariance (see equations 19 through 21), except that the error term is that for the randomized complete block design and has N−n−k degrees of freedom instead of N−k−1, and the various sums of squares of X are those computed for the randomized complete block design.

NUMERIC EXAMPLE FOR
RANDOMIZED COMPLETE BLOCK DESIGN

In the example accompanying the completely randomized design, researchers were concerned with the impact of the establishment of a package liquor store, alone or with a licensed restaurant, on the rate of traffic accidents in rural municipalities. Assume that illustration to have been an experimental study, and that before the experiment was conducted it was suspected that certain subcultural differences among the various geographic regions of the country might have some impact upon the dependent variable. In order to control for this possible source of variablility and, thereby, increase the precision of the experiment, one test unit (rural municipality) from each of the country's four geographical/subcultural regions was randomly assigned to each of the three treatment levels. The data resulting from this experiment are presented in Table 7.

The experimental setting, with the above described modification, represents a randomized complete block design. As with the completely randomized design, the primary purpose is to test the hypothesis that all levels of liquor licensing have equal impact on the rate of traffic accidents. This hypothesis is tested with an F-ratio (equation 44) which requires the following computations:

(1) compute the error sums of squares and cross products, E_{xx}, E_{xy} and E_{yy} (refer to Table 6 for appropriate equations for this and subsequent computations),

(2) compute the treatment sums of squares and cross products, B_{xx}, B_{xy} and B_{yy},

(3) compute the adjusted error and treatment sums of squares, $E_{yy(adj)}$ and $B_{yy(adj)}$, and

(4) compute the F-ratio.

The numeric results of these computations for the present example are presented in Table 8. The computed F-ratio is 41.20 which is significant

TABLE 7
Data for Randomized Complete Block Design: Traffic Accidents During the Test Period (Y) and Traffic Accidents During Preceding Year (X)

Geographic Regions (Blocks)	Type of Liquor Licensing (Treatment or Groups)						Block Means	
	Control (Group 1)		Store Only (Group 2)		Restaurant and Package Store (Group 3)			
	X	Y	X	Y	X	Y	$\bar{X}_J$	$\bar{Y}_J$
A	190	177	252	226	206	226	216.00	209.67
B	261	225	228	196	239	229	242.67	216.67
C	194	167	240	198	217	215	217.00	193.33
D	217	176	246	206	177	188	213.33	190.00
Treatment Means	215.50	186.25	241.50	206.50	209.75	214.50		

Sample Means $\bar{X} = 222.50$ $\bar{Y} = 202.42$

[65]

TABLE 8

Analysis of Covariance for Randomized Complete Block Design with Data From Illustrative Example

Source of Variation	Sum of Squares and Cross Products			Adjusted Sum of Squares	Degrees of Freedom	Adjusted Mean Square	F-ratio
	XX	XY	YY				
Blocks	1688.42	1212.54	1476.92	607.37	3	202.34	7.16
Treatments	2289.50	146.75	1696.17	2329.01	2	1164.51	41.20
Error	3805.83	2794.92	2193.83	141.31	5	28.26	
Total					10		

at $\alpha = .05$ ($F_{.05;2,5} = 5.79$). Therefore, the null hypothesis is rejected, implying that the treatment levels do have differential effects. The exact nature of these effects will be examined shortly.

Block effects are tested (i.e., test the hypothesis that $R_j = 0$ for all j) using the F-ratio (equation 46) of adjusted mean square for blocks to adjusted mean square error. The computations (refer to Table 6) for this test are completed as follows:

(1) compute the block sums of squares and cross products, S_{xx}, S_{xy} and S_{yy},

(2) compute the adjusted block sum of squares $S_{yy(adj)}$ (note, the error and adjusted error sums of squares have been calculated in conjunction with the test of treatment effects), and

(3) compute the F-ratio.

The numeric result of the computations outlined above are presented in Table 8, and the calculated F-ratio of 7.16 is significant at $\alpha.05$ ($F_{.05;3,5} = 5.41$). Therefore the null hypothesis of no block effects is rejected.

At this point, the assumption that the coefficient of the covariate is nonzero is considered. The null hypothesis in this case is that $\beta = 0$ and the test statistic (equation 47) is the F-ratio:

$$F = E_{xy}^2(N-n-k)/(E_{yy}E_{xx} - E_{xy}^2)$$

$$= (2794.92)^2 (12-4-3)/[(2193.83)(3805.83) - (2794.92)^2]$$

$$= 72.62.$$

Given this F-value, the hypothesis that $\beta = 0$ is rejected ($F_{.05;1,5} = 6.61$), and the hypothesized model is consistent with the observed data.

The test for homogeneity of regression is easily conducted using the "added sum of squares" principle (see pp. 45-49), which results in a comparison of the standard randomized complete block covariance model (equation 39) and a similar model with three separate regression coefficients, one for each treatment level. That test gives a calculated F-ratio of 2.72, and there is no reason to reject the hypothesis of homogeneity of regression ($F_{.10;2,3} = 5.46$).

For purposes of interpretation it is useful to calculate the pooled within class regression coefficient,

$$b_w = E_{xy}/E_{xx} = 2794.92/3805.83 = 0.7344,$$

and the adjusted group means,

$$\bar{Y}_{1 \cdot (adj)} = \bar{Y}_1. - b_w(\bar{X}_1. - \bar{X}) = 186.25 - 0.7344(215.50 - 222.25)$$

$$= 191.21,$$

$$\bar{Y}_{2 \cdot (adj)} = \bar{Y}_2. - b_w(\bar{X}_2. - \bar{X}) = 206.50 - 0.7344(241.50 - 222.25)$$

$$= 192.36,$$

and

$$\bar{Y}_{3 \cdot (adj)} = \bar{Y}_3. - b_w(\bar{X}_3. - \bar{X}) = 214.50 - 0.7344(209.75 - 222.25)$$

$$= 223.68.$$

The same mean comparisons that were computed in conjunction with the numeric example for the completely randomized design are now considered. The a priori comparison of group 1 and group 3, control group and treatment group with both package store and licensed restaurant respectively, is tested with the t-statistic given by equation 19 with the values of $\bar{Y}_{i(adj)}$, $MSE_{(adj)}$ and E_{xx} being those computed for the randomized complete block design. The calculated t-value is -8.56, and the null hypothesis of no difference is rejected ($t_{.05,5} = 2.57$). It is concluded that the accident rate is higher in the treatment group than in the control group. The a posteriori pairwise comparisons of all means (Tukey's HSD procedure) are computed by substituting the appropriate quantities from the randomized complete block design into equation 20. The resulting q-values are -10.71, $-.43$ and -10.28 for treatment 1 with 3, treatment 1 with 2 and treatment 2 with 3, respectively. Given these calculated q-values, the null hypothesis of no difference is rejected for the comparisons of treatment 1 and treatment 2 with treatment 3 ($q_{.05,5,3} = 4.60$), but cannot be rejected for the comparison of treatment 1 with treatment 2.

The reader should note that the results of the analysis for the randomized complete block design are quite similar to those for the completely randomized design. The major difference is the considerable decrease in the error sum of squares (note also the decrease in the associated degrees of freedom) for the randomized complete block design. This will occur whenever blocking is employed as long as the test unit characteristics used to define the blocks are significantly related to the dependent variable. Accompanying this decrease in the error sum of squares is an increase in the calculated F- and t-statistics.

Factorial Design

Often, interest centers on the simultaneous evaluation of two or more categorical independent variables in a single analysis. Many cases such as this exist and a variety of designs, all included under the general classification of factorial designs, are available to handle them. In these cases, the researcher is simultaneously interested in the effect of all categorical independent variables, and the test units are typically randomly assigned to the various combinations of levels of the categorical independent variables by the researcher. This differs from the randomized block design just discussed in that with that design, the test unit characteristics are not under the control of the researcher, could not be randomly assigned, and were not of primary interest to the researcher. However, the analysis procedures for the two types of designs can be similar.

Factorial designs may include more than two independent variables, and employ a number of variations in the assignment of test units. When a quantitative independent variable (covariate) is considered in addition to the categorical independent variables, the analysis procedure employed is a factorial analysis of covariance. The design considered here is the simplest of factorial designs, the two-factor balanced factorial analysis of covariance design. This design considers two categorical independent variables, the first (designated factor A) with p levels and the second (factor B) with q levels, pq treatment combinations with an equal number of test units randomly assigned to each, and one covariate. The two-factor factorial with an unequal number of test units per treatment combination is discussed at the conclusion of the factorial design section (pages 86-87). For a discussion of more complex factorial designs the reader is referred to Ostle (1963) or Kirk (1968).

Before proceeding, it should be mentioned that the two-factor balanced factorial analysis of covariance procedure is equally applicable to observational studies and experimental studies. However, the number of observational studies in which there occurs an equal number of observations for each cell (combination of levels of two categorical variables) is limited. Observational studies tend to have unequal cell sizes and should be analyzed accordingly.

COVARIANCE MODEL

The linear model for the completely randomized factorial analysis of covariance with two factors and one covariate is,

$$Y_{ijk} = u + \alpha_i + \gamma_j + (\alpha\gamma)_{ij} + \beta(X_{ijk} - \overline{X}) + e_{ijk}; \quad i=1,\ldots,p; \quad j=1,\ldots,q;$$
$$\text{and } k=1,\ldots,n; \qquad [48]$$

where Y_{ijk} is the observed value of the dependent variable for the kth observation within the ith level of factor A and the jth level of factor B, u is the true mean effect, α_i is the effect due to the ith level of factor A with $\Sigma\alpha_i = 0$, γ_j is the effect due to the jth level of factor B with $\Sigma\gamma_j = 0$, $(\alpha\gamma)_{ij}$ is the effect due to the interaction of the ith level of factor A with the jth level of factor B with $\Sigma_i(\alpha\gamma)_{ij} = 0$ and $\Sigma_j(\alpha\gamma)_{ij} = 0$, β is the (regression) coefficient of the covariate, X_{ijk} is the observed value of the covariate, $\overline{X}$ is the general mean of the covariate, and e_{ijk} is the random error which is normally and independently distributed with mean zero and variance σ^2.

For the completely randomized factorial design, primary interest lies in examining the differences in the effects of the various levels of the categorical independent variables (factors) and their interactions. As with the designs previously considered, the hypotheses of no effect due to factors and interaction are tested using F-ratios of adjusted mean squares. The procedures for calculating the necessary adjusted sums of squares for the two-factor factorial analysis of covariance are considered below.

The adjusted error sum of squres of Y, $E_{yy(adj)}$, for the factorial design is obtained in a manner directly analogous to that used for the completely randomized and the randomized complete block designs. The computational equation for $E_{yy(adj)}$ is;

$$E_{yy(adj)} = E_{yy} - b_w^2 E_{xx} = E_{yy} - E_{xy}^2/E_{xx} \qquad [49]$$

where;

$$E_{yy} = \sum_{i=1}^{p}\sum_{j=1}^{q}\sum_{k=1}^{n}(Y_{ijk} - \overline{Y}_{ij})^2,$$

$$E_{xy} = \sum_{i=1}^{p}\sum_{j=1}^{q}\sum_{k=1}^{n}(X_{ijk} - \overline{X}_{ij})(Y_{ijk} - \overline{Y}_{ij}),$$

$$E_{xx} = \sum_{i=1}^{p}\sum_{j=1}^{q}\sum_{k=1}^{n}(X_{ijk} - \overline{X}_{ij})^2, \text{ and}$$

$$b_w = E_{xy}/E_{xx},$$

with $\overline{Y}_{ij}$ and $\overline{X}_{ij}$ equal to the mean values of Y_{ijk} and X_{ijk}, respectively, for the i*th* level of factor A and the j*th* level of factor B. The degrees of freedom for $E_{yy(adj)}$ are $N-pq-1$.

The adjusted factor and interaction sums of squares of Y for the factorial analysis of covariance are computed in the same manner as the adjusted treatment sum of squares of Y in the randomized complete block design. First, consider factor A.

If it were assumed that the factor A effects are zero, i.e., $\alpha_i = 0$ for all i, then the adjusted error sum of squares of Y would be computed as:

$$E^*_{yy(adj)} = E^*_{yy} - E^{*2}_{xy}/E^*_{xx} \qquad [50]$$

where;

$$E^*_{yy} = \sum_{i=1}^{p} \sum_{j=1}^{q} \sum_{k=1}^{n} (Y_{ijk} - \overline{Y}_{\cdot j})^2,$$

$$E^*_{xy} = \sum_{i=1}^{p} \sum_{j=1}^{q} \sum_{k=1}^{n} (X_{ijk} - \overline{X}_{\cdot j})(Y_{ijk} - \overline{Y}_{\cdot j}), \text{ and}$$

$$E^*_{xx} = \sum_{i=1}^{p} \sum_{j=1}^{q} \sum_{k=1}^{n} (X_{ijk} - \overline{X}_{\cdot j})^2,$$

with $\overline{Y}_{\cdot j}$ and $\overline{X}_{\cdot j}$ equal to the mean values of Y_{ijk} and X_{ijk}, respectively, for the j*th* level of factor B. Now, if the assumption that factor A effects are zero is not valid, $E^*_{yy(adj)}$ consists of both factor A effects and error effects. But, by subtracting out the error effects, as computed by equation 49, the remainder would be the factor A effects. Therefore, the adjusted factor A sum of squares of Y, $A_{yy(adj)}$, is obtained by subtraction,

$$A_{yy(adj)} = E^*_{yy(adj)} - E_{yy(adj)}. \qquad [51]$$

Further, it can be shown that

$$E^*_{yy} = A_{yy} + E_{yy},$$

$$E^*_{xy} = A_{xy} + E_{xy}, \text{ and}$$

$$E^*_{xx} = A_{xx} + E_{xx}$$

where;

$$A_{yy} = qn \sum_{i=1}^{p} (\bar{Y}_{i\cdot} - \bar{Y})^2,$$

$$A_{xy} = qn \sum_{i=1}^{p} (\bar{X}_{i\cdot} - \bar{X})(\bar{Y}_{i\cdot} - \bar{Y}), \text{ and}$$

$$A_{xx} = qn \sum_{i=1}^{p} (\bar{X}_{i\cdot} - \bar{X})^2,$$

with $\bar{Y}_{i\cdot}$ and $\bar{X}_{i\cdot}$ equal to the mean values of Y_{ijk} and X_{ijk}, respectively, for the i*th* level of factor A. Using these relationships, equation 51 is expressed:

$$A_{yy(adj)} = (A_{yy} + E_{yy}) - (A_{xy} + E_{xy})^2/(A_{xx} + E_{xx}) - E_{yy(adj)}. \qquad [52]$$

The degrees of freedom for $A_{yy(adj)}$ are (N−pq+p−2)−(N−pq−1) = p−1, the difference in the degrees of freedom of the terms in equation 51.

The adjusted factor B sum of squares of Y, $B_{yy(adj)}$, and the adjusted interaction sum of squares of Y, $AB_{yy(adj)}$, are obtained in a like manner. For factor B,

$$B_{yy(adj)} = (B_{yy} + E_{yy}) - (B_{xy} + E_{xy})^2/(B_{xx} + E_{xx}) - E_{yy(adj)} \qquad [53]$$

where,

$$B_{yy} = pn \sum_{j=1}^{q} (\bar{Y}_{\cdot j} - \bar{Y})^2,$$

$$B_{xy} = pn \sum_{j=1}^{q} (\bar{X}_{\cdot j} - \bar{X})(\bar{Y}_{\cdot j} - \bar{Y}), \text{ and}$$

$$B_{xx} = pn \sum_{j=1}^{q} (\bar{X}_{\cdot j} - \bar{X})^2.$$

The degrees of freedom for $B_{yy(adj)}$ are $(N-pq+q-2) - (N-pq-1) = q-1$. For the interaction,

$$AB_{yy(adj)} = (AB_{yy} + E_{yy}) - (AB_{xy} + E_{xy})^2/(AB_{xx} + E_{xx}) \qquad [54]$$
$$- E_{yy(adj)}$$

where,

$$AB_{yy} = n \sum_{i=1}^{p} \sum_{j=1}^{q} (\bar{Y}_{ij} - \bar{Y}_{i\bullet} - \bar{Y}_{\bullet j} + \bar{Y})^2,$$

$$AB_{xy} = n \sum_{i=1}^{p} \sum_{j=1}^{q} (\bar{X}_{ij} - \bar{X}_{i\bullet} - \bar{X}_{\bullet j} + \bar{X}) (\bar{Y}_{ij} - \bar{Y}_{i\bullet} - \bar{Y}_{\bullet j} + \bar{Y}), \text{ and}$$

$$AB_{xx} = n \sum_{i=1}^{p} \sum_{j=1}^{q} (\bar{X}_{ij} - \bar{X}_{i\bullet} - \bar{X}_{\bullet j} + \bar{X})^2.$$

The degrees of freedom for $AB_{yy(adj)}$ are

$$(N-p-q) - (N-pq-1) = (p-1) (q-1).$$

For this two-factor factorial design there are three major hypotheses of interest. In each case an F-ratio is the appropriate test statistic. The first hypothesis considered is the null hypothesis of no factor A effects, i.e., $\alpha_i = 0$ for all i. The test statistic is the F-ratio,

$$F_A = \frac{A_{yy(adj)}/(p-1)}{E_{yy(adj)}/(N-pq-1)} \qquad [55]$$

which under the null hypothesis has an F-distribution with $p-1$ and $N-pq-1$ degrees of freedom. The next hypothesis is the null hypothesis of no factor B effects, i.e., $\gamma_j = 0$ for all j. The test statistic is the F-ratio,

$$F_B = \frac{B_{yy(adj)}/(q-1)}{E_{yy(adj)}/(N-pq-1)} \qquad [56]$$

which under the null hypothesis has an F-distribution with q-1 and N-pq-1 degrees of freedom. The third hypothesis is that of no interaction effect, i.e., $(\alpha\gamma)_{ij} = 0$ for all i and j. The test statistic is the F-ratio,

$$F_{AB} = \frac{AB_{yy(adj)}/(p-1)(q-1)}{E_{yy(adj)}/(N-pq-1)} \qquad [57]$$

which under the null hypothesis has an F-distribution with (p-1)(q-1) and N-pq-1 degrees of freedom. The analysis of covariance table for the two-factor factorial design is presented in Table 9.

If there is only one test unit per treatment combination, i.e., n = 1, the interaction effects, $(\alpha\gamma)_{ij}$, are assumed to be zero, the adjusted error sum of squares is computed according to equation 40, and the computations and test associated with the interaction are deleted.

FURTHER CONSIDERATIONS

In the presence of a significant interaction effect, the interpretation of a statistically significant factor effect may become very complex. Under these circumstances, the significance of a factor indicates that significant differences in the dependent variable exist on average (averaged over levels of the other factor) across the levels of that significant factor. But, for any given level of the other factor, the differences in the dependent variable over the levels of that significant factor may, or may not, be themselves statistically significant. This suggests the usefulness of testing the significance of one factor while holding the other factor constant at given levels. Tests of this type are referred to as tests of *simple* main effects.

If a significant interaction effect is found, added insight into the nature of the experimental results can be gained through an examination of the simple main effects. Simple main effect tests for a two-factor factorial design, in the case of factor A, tests the null hypothesis that the factor A effect is zero over a specified level of factor B, i.e., $\alpha_i = 0$ for all i given j = J, and, for factor B, test the null hypothesis that the factor B effect is zero over a specified level of factor A, i.e., $\gamma_j = 0$ for all j given i = I. In order to conduct these tests it is necessary to compute adjusted factor sums of squares of Y for one factor while holding the other factor constant at the specified level. The computation of these adjusted sums of squares is discussed below.

TABLE 9
Analysis of Covariance for Two-Factor Factorial Design

Source of Variation	Sum of Squares and Cross Products			Adjusted Sum of Squares	Degrees of Freedom	Adjusted Mean Square	Expected Mean Square	F-Ratio
	XX	XY	YY					
Treatment A	A_{xx}	A_{xy}	A_{yy}	$A_{YY(ADJ)}$	$P-1$	$\dfrac{A_{YY(ADJ)}}{P-1}$	$\sigma^2_{\epsilon\mid\beta} + \dfrac{QN\Sigma\alpha^2_I}{P-1}$	$\dfrac{MSA(ADJ)}{MSE(ADJ)}$
Treatment B	B_{xx}	B_{xy}	B_{yy}	$B_{YY(ADJ)}$	$Q-1$	$\dfrac{B_{YY(ADJ)}}{Q-1}$	$\sigma^2_{\epsilon\mid\beta} + \dfrac{PN\Sigma\gamma^2_I}{Q-1}$	$\dfrac{MSB(ADJ)}{MSE(ADJ)}$
Interaction	AB_{xx}	AB_{xy}	AB_{yy}	$AB_{YY(ADJ)}$	$(P-1)(Q-1)$	$\dfrac{AB_{YY(ADJ)}}{(P-1)(Q-1)}$	$\sigma^2_{\epsilon\mid\beta} + \dfrac{N\Sigma\Sigma(\alpha\gamma)^2_I}{(P-1)(Q-1)}$	$\dfrac{MSAB(ADJ)}{MSE(ADJ)}$
Error	E_{xx}	E_{xy}	E_{yy}	$E_{YY(ADJ)}$	$N-PQ-1$	$\dfrac{E_{YY(ADJ)}}{N-PQ-1}$	$\sigma^2_{\epsilon\mid\beta}$	
Total					$N-2$			

$A_{xx} = qn\Sigma(\overline{X}_{i.} - \overline{X})^2$

$A_{xy} = qn\Sigma(\overline{X}_{i.} - \overline{X})(\overline{Y}_{i.} - \overline{Y})$

$A_{yy} = qn\Sigma(\overline{Y}_{i.} - \overline{Y})^2$

$B_{xx} = pn\Sigma(\overline{X}_{.j} - \overline{X})^2$

$B_{xy} = pn\Sigma(\overline{X}_{.j} - \overline{X})(\overline{Y}_{.j} - \overline{Y})$

$B_{yy} = pn\Sigma(\overline{Y}_{.j} - \overline{Y})^2$

$AB_{xx} = n\Sigma\Sigma(\overline{X}_{ij} - \overline{X}_{i.} - \overline{X}_{.j} + \overline{X})^2$

$AB_{yy} = n\Sigma\Sigma(\overline{Y}_{ij} - \overline{Y}_{i.} - \overline{Y}_{.j} + \overline{Y})^2$

$AB_{yy} = n\Sigma\Sigma(\overline{Y}_{ij} - \overline{Y}_{i.} - \overline{Y}_{.j} + \overline{Y})^2$

$E_{xx} = \Sigma\Sigma\Sigma(X_{ijk} - \overline{X}_{ij})^2$

$E_{xy} = \Sigma\Sigma\Sigma(X_{ijk} - \overline{X}_{ij})(Y_{ijk} - \overline{Y}_{ij})$

$E_{yy} = \Sigma\Sigma\Sigma(Y_{ijk} - \overline{Y}_{ij})^2$

$E_{yy(adj)} = E_{yy} - E^2_{xy}/E_{xx}$

$A_{yy(adj)} = (A_{yy} + E_{yy}) - (A_{xy} + E_{xy})^2/(A_{xx} + E_{xx}) - E_{yy(adj)}$

$B_{yy(adj)} = (B_{yy} + E_{yy}) - (B_{xy} + E_{xy})^2/(B_{xx} + E_{xx}) - E_{yy(adj)}$

$AB_{yy(adj)} = (AB_{yy} + E_{yy}) - (AB_{xy} + E_{xy})^2/(AB_{xx} + E_{xx}) - E_{yy(adj)}$

The adjusted factor A sum of squares of Y at level B_j, designated $A_{yy(adj,B_j)}$, is computed as follows:

$$A_{yy(adj,B_j)} = (A_{yy(B_j)} + E_{yy}) - (A_{xy(B_j)} + E_{xy})^2 / (A_{xx(B_j)} + E_{xx})$$
$$- E_{yy(adj)} \qquad [58]$$

where,

$$A_{yy(B_j)} = n \sum_{i=1}^{p} (\bar{Y}_{ij} - \bar{Y}_{\cdot j})^2,$$

$$A_{xy(B_j)} = n \sum_{i=1}^{p} (\bar{X}_{ij} - \bar{X}_{\cdot j}) (\bar{Y}_{ij} - \bar{Y}_{\cdot j}), \text{ and}$$

$$A_{xx(B_j)} = n \sum_{i=1}^{p} (\bar{X}_{ij} - \bar{X}_{\cdot j})^2.$$

The degrees of freedom for $A_{yy(adj,B_j)}$ are $p-1$. The adjusted factor B sum of squares at level A_i is computed in a like manner:

$$B_{yy(adj,A_i)} = (B_{yy(A_i)} + E_{yy}) - (B_{xy(A_i)} + E_{xy})^2 / (B_{xx(A_i)} + E_{xx})$$
$$- E_{yy(adj)} \qquad [59]$$

where,

$$B_{yy(A_i)} = n \sum_{j=1}^{q} (\bar{Y}_{ij} - \bar{Y}_{i\cdot})^2,$$

$$B_{xy(A_i)} = n \sum_{j=1}^{q} (\bar{X}_{ij} - \bar{X}_{i\cdot}) (\bar{Y}_{ij} - \bar{Y}_{i\cdot}), \text{ and}$$

$$B_{xx(A_i)} = n \sum_{j=1}^{q} (\bar{X}_{ij} - \bar{X}_{i\cdot})^2.$$

The degrees of freedom for $B_{yy(adj,A_j)}$ are $q-1$.

The test statistic for the factor A null hypothesis, $\alpha_i = 0$ for all i at level B_j, is the F-ratio

$$F_{A(B_j)} = \frac{A_{yy(adj,B_j)}/(p-1)}{E_{yy(adj)}/(N-pq-1)} \qquad [60]$$

which under the null hypothesis has an F-distribution with $p-1$ and $N-pq-1$ degrees of freedom. It is recommended to assign the same error rate for the *set* of simple main effects as that determined for the overall F-ratio. Thus, if the level of significance is selected to be $\alpha = .05$ for the overall test, the simple main effect ratios for treatment A should be tested at the $.05/q$ level of significance.

To test the factor B null hypothesis, $\gamma_j = 0$ for all j at A_i, the calculated F-ratio is:

$$F_{B(A_i)} = \frac{B_{yy(adj,A_i)}/(q-1)}{E_{yy(adj)}/(N-pq-1)} \qquad [61]$$

which under the null hypothesis has an F-distribution with $q-1$ and $N-pq-1$ degrees of freedom. The recommended significance level is α/p where α is the significance level selected for the overall test.

TESTING β

The covariance model assumes the within cell regression coefficients are equal for all combinations of factors A *and* B. The hypothesis of homogeneity of regression is tested with an F-statistic, similar to that used in the completely randomized design. The test statistic is:

$$F = \frac{(E_{yy(adj)} - S_1)/(pq-1)}{S_1/(N-2pq)} \qquad [62]$$

where $E_{yy(adj)}$ is given by equation 49 and,

$$S_1 = E_{yy} - \sum_{i=1}^{p} \sum_{j=1}^{q} b_{w_{ij}}^2 E_{xx_{ij}} \qquad [63]$$

where E_{yy} is the error sum of squares of Y for the factorial design, $b_{w_{ij}} = E_{xy_{ij}}/E_{xx_{ij}}$ is the within cell regression coefficient for the ith level of factor A and the jth level of factor B, $E_{xy_{ij}} = \Sigma_k(X_{ijk} - \bar{X}_{ij})(Y_{ijk} - \bar{Y}_{ij})$ is the error sum of squares for the cross product of X and Y for the ith level of factor A and the jth level of factor B, and $E_{xx_{ij}} = \Sigma_k(X_{ijk} - \bar{X}_{ij})^2$ is the error sum of squares of X for the ith level of factor A and the jth level of factor B. Under the null hypothesis of homogeneity of within cell regression, this test statistic is distributed as the F-distribution with pq−1 and N−2pq degrees of freedom.

The test statistic for the hypothesis that $\beta = 0$ is given by,

$$F = E_{xy}^2(N-pq-1)/(E_{yy}E_{xx} - E_{xy}^2) \qquad [64]$$

where the error sums of squares have been defined in relation to equation 49. Under the null hypothesis this test statistic is distributed as the F-distribution with 1 and N−pq−1 degrees of freedom.

COMPARISONS AMONG MEANS

A significant F-ratio for a main effect (factor A or factor B) in a two-factor factorial design indicates that at least one level of that main effect is different from the others. As with the other designs discussed, further investigation into the nature of these differences requires the use of mean comparisons, and, as with the other designs, these mean comparisons utilize adjusted group means. However, for the factorial design it is sometimes useful to differentiate between two types of mean comparisons. The first is designated a main effect mean comparison and compares means for different levels of one factor where the means are averaged over all levels of the other factor. The second is referred to as a *simple* main effect mean comparison and compares means for different levels of one factor within a single level of the other factor, i.e., compares cell means while holding one of the factors constant. The reason for having these two types of comparisons is that when the interaction effect is significant, tests of differences among means for main effects are often of little interest, and, the interesting findings are sought by comparisons among *simple* main effects.

The adjusted means for these two types of comparisons are computed as follows:

$$\bar{Y}_{(adj)}^{(k)} = \bar{Y}^{(k)} - b_w(\bar{X}^{(k)} - \bar{X}) \qquad [65]$$

where $b_w = E_{xy}/E_{xx}$ is the pooled within cell regression coefficient, and $\overline{Y}^{(k)}$ and $\overline{X}^{(k)}$ are equal to $\overline{Y}_{i.}$ and $\overline{X}_{i.}$, $\overline{Y}_{.j}$ and $\overline{X}_{.j}$, and $\overline{Y}_{ij}$ and $\overline{X}_{ij}$ for main effect factor A, main effect factor B and simple main effect comparisons, respectively.

A priori orthogonal comparisons among means for both main effects and simple main effects are given by

$$t = \frac{\Sigma c_k \overline{Y}^{(k)}_{(adj)}}{\sqrt{MSE_{(adj)}\left[\Sigma(c_k^2/n_k) + [\Sigma c_k(\overline{X}^{(k)} - \overline{X})]^2/E_{xx}\right]}} \qquad [66]$$

where $\overline{Y}_{(adj)}$ and $\overline{X}^{(k)}$ are defined as above, and n_k is nq and np respectively for factor A and B main effect comparisons, and n for simple main effect comparisons. Under the hypothesis of no difference this ratio has a t-distribution with N−pq−1 degrees of freedom. (It should be kept in mind that when testing *simple* main effect comparisons the level of significance should be set a α/q and α/p for A and B, respectively.)

For unplanned, a posteriori, pairwise comparisons, Tukey's (HSD) test is computed:

$$q = \frac{c_k \overline{Y}^{(k)}_{(adj)} + c_{k'} \overline{Y}^{(k')}_{(adj)}}{\sqrt{\dfrac{MSE_{(adj)}}{n_k}\; 1 + \left[\dfrac{K_{xx}}{[d.f.(K)]\,E_{xx}}\right]}} \qquad [67]$$

where $\overline{Y}^{(k)}_{(adj)}$ and n_k are defined as above, K_{xx} equals A_{xx}, B_{xx} and AB_{xx} respectively for factor A and B main effect comparisons and simple main effect comparisons, and d.f. (K) is the degrees of freedom associated with $K_{yy(adj)}$. The corresponding a posteriori test using Scheffe's procedure results in the following test statistic:

$$F = \frac{\Sigma c_k \overline{Y}^{(k)}_{(adj)}}{MSE_{(adj)}\left[1 + \dfrac{K_{xx}}{[d.f.(K)]\,E_{xx}}\right]\left[\Sigma(c_k^2/n_k)\right]} \cdot \frac{1}{(m_k - 1)} \qquad [68]$$

where m_k is the total number of means from which the specific comparison is formed, and the other quantities are defined above. This F-value is compared to the critical value from the F-distribution with d.f.(K) and N−pq−1 degrees of freedom. (Again it is noted that the significance levels should be adjusted for simple main effect comparisons.)

NUMERIC EXAMPLE FOR TWO-FACTOR DESIGN WITH EQUAL CELL SIZE

In the example provided for the completely randomized design, researchers were concerned with the impact of three levels of liquor licensing (no liquor sold, package store only, and both package store and licensed restaurant) on the rate of traffic accidents in rural municipalities. Now, assume that a fourth treatment level, licensed restaurant only, is added to the initial design and all treatment levels are randomly assigned to four rural municipalities. With the addition of this fourth group the study may be conceptualized as a two-by-two factorial design, where factor A is the establishment of a package store (two levels: yes or no), and factor B is the establishment of a licensed restaurant (two levels: yes or no). The data from this study are presented in Table 10.

As was the case with the previous analyses, the primary purpose is to test the impact of the various treatment combinations on the dependent variable. With the two-factor factorial design this is accomplished by testing three hypotheses; one concerning factor A, a second concerning factor B, and the third concerning the interaction of factors A and B. Each of these hypotheses is tested with an F-ratio (see equations 55-57). The F-ratios require the calculation of the adjusted sums of squares of Y, $E_{yy(adj)}$, $A_{yy(adj)}$, $B_{yy(adj)}$ and $AB_{yy(adj)}$ (see equations 49, 52-54), which in turn require the computation of twelve sums of squares and cross product terms (E_{xx}, E_{xy}, E_{yy}, A_{xx}, A_{xy}, A_{yy}, B_{xx}, B_{xy}, B_{yy}, AB_{xx}, AB_{xy} and AB_{yy}). The calculated values of the F-ratios, the adjusted sums of squares of Y, and the sums of squares and cross products are reported in Table 11. The three F-ratios are all significant at the α = .05 level ($F_{.05;1,11}$ = 4.84), therefore, all three null hypotheses are rejected.

Some researchers consider it preferable to test for interaction effects first, and if they are found to be significant proceed directly to test the simple main effect hypotheses. The merit of this approach is the simplicity of interpretation of simple main effect tests, as compared to main effect tests, in the presence of a significant interaction. For the present example there are four simple main effect hypotheses, each of which are examined, with summary results presented in Table 12.

TABLE 10
Data for Two-Factor Factorial Design:
Traffice Accidents During Test Period (Y) and
Traffic Accidents During Preceding Year (X)

Licensed Restaurant (Factor B)	Package Store (Factor A)				Factor B Means	
	Yes (Level 1)		No (Level 2)			
	X	Y	X	Y	X	Y
Yes (Level 1)	206	226	248	229		
	239	229	208	190		
	217	215	225	195		
	177	188	239	202		
Means	209.75	214.50	230.00	204.00	219.88	209.25
No (Level 2)	252	226	190	177		
	228	196	261	225		
	240	198	194	167		
	246	206	217	176		
Means	241.50	206.50	215.50	186.25	228.50	196.38
Factor A Means	225.63	210.50	222.75	195.13		

Sample Means $\bar{X}$ = 224.19 $\bar{Y}$ = 202.81

The first simple main effect hypothesis considered is H_o: α_i = 0 for all i at level B_1; i.e., given a licensed restaurant is established, there is no difference in the traffic accident rate whether or not a package store is also established. The F-value (calculated using equation 60) to test this hypothesis is 12.91. $F_{.025;1,11}$ = 6.72, therefore, the null hypotheses that the addition of the package store does not make any difference given a licensed restaurant is established, is rejected. The second hypothesis tested is H_o: α_i = 0 for all i at level B_2; i.e., given a licensed restaurant is not established, there is no difference in the traffic accident rate whether or not a package store is established. The calculated F-ratio is 0.004. This ratio is far from significant and, therefore, one cannot reject the null hypothesis that the addition of the package store does *not* make any difference given a

TABLE 11

Analysis of Covariance for Factorial Design with Data From Illustrative Example

Source of Variation	Sum of Squares and Cross Products			Adjusted Sum of Squares	Degrees of Freedom	Adjusted Mean Square	F-ratio
	XX	XY	YY				
Factor A	33.06	176.81	945.56	696.04	1	696.04	7.71
Factor B	297.56	-444.19	663.06	1427.42	1	1427.42	15.80
Interaction	2139.06	450.94	95.06	462.51	1	462.51	5.12
Error	6408.75	4792.00	4576.75	993.64	11	90.33	
Total					14		

TABLE 12
Analysis of Simple Main Effects for Factorial Design
with Data From Illustrative Example

Source of Variation	Sum of Squares and Cross Products			Adjusted Sum of Squares	Degrees of Freedom	F-ratio
	XX	XY	YY			
Factor A at B_1	820.13	-425.25	220.50	1165.79	1	12.91
Factor A at B_2	1352.00	1053.00	820.13	1.08	1	0.004
Factor B at A_1	2016.13	-508.00	128.00	1532.72	1	16.97
Factor B at A_2	420.50	514.75	630.13	89.56	1	0.99
Error				993.64	11	

licensed restaurant is *not* established. The third hypothesis tested is H_o: $\gamma_j = 0$ for all j at level A_1; i.e., given a package store is established, there is no difference in the accident rate if the licensed restaurant is established or not. The F-value, calculated using equation 61, is 16.97. Since $F_{.025;1,11} = 6.72$, the null hypotheses that the addition of the licensed restaurant does not make any difference given a package store is established, is rejected. The final simple main effect hypothesis tested is H_o: $\gamma_j = 0$ for all j at level A_2; i.e., given a package store is not established, there is no difference in the accident rate if a licensed restaurant is established or not. The computed F-value of 0.99 is not significant and one cannot reject the null hypothesis that the addition of the licensed restaurant does *not* have any effect on the traffic accident rate given a package store is *not* established. In summary, establishing either package store or licensed restaurant alone did not seem to have significant impact on traffic accident rates, but if both are established in a municipality the effect is significant.

The covariance model assumes equality of within cell regression coefficients. The test of this assumption of homogeneity of regression is given by equation 62, which requires the calculation of the error sum of squares of X for each cell, $E_{xx_{ij}}$, and the within cell regresion coefficients, $b_{w_{ij}} = E_{xy_{ij}}/E_{xx_{ij}}$, where $E_{xy_{ij}}$ is the error sum of squares for the cross product of X and Y for cell ij. The computation of these quantities for cells 11, 12 and 22 has already been completed in conjunction with the numeric example for the completely randomized design (see pages 37-38; cells 11, 12 and 22 correspond to treatments 3, 2 and 1 of the completely randomized design, respectively). These quantities are similarly calculated for cell 21. The resulting values are: $E_{xy_{21}} = 785.00$, $E_{xx_{21}} = 914.00$ and $b_{w_{21}} = 0.8589$. The calculated F-value is 0.255 and the hypothesis of homogeneity of regression ($F_{.10;3,8} = 2.92$) is not rejected.

The second assumption tested is that the regression coefficient is non-zero. The test statistic (computed using equation 64) for the null hypothesis that $\beta = 0$ is 13.465. Given this F-ratio, the hypothesis that $\beta = 0$ is rejected ($F_{.05;1,11} = 4.84$), and the hypothesized model is consistent with the observed data.

In the presence of a significant interaction effect it is usually helpful to graphically present the results. In order to do this the pooled within cell regression coefficient, b_w, and the adjusted cell means, $\overline{Y}_{ij(adj)}$, must be obtained. These quantities are computed as follows:

$$b_w = E_{xy}/E_{xx} = 4792.00/6408.75 = 0.7477,$$

$$\overline{Y}_{11(adj)} = \overline{Y}_{11} - b_w(\overline{X}_{11} - \overline{X}) = 214.50 - 0.7477(209.75 - 224.19)$$

$$= 225.29,$$

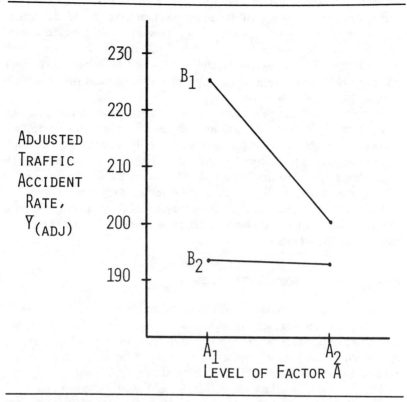

Figure 5: Adjusted Treatment Means

$$\overline{Y}_{12(adj)} = \overline{Y}_{12} - b_w(\overline{X}_{12} - \overline{X}) = 206.50 - 0.7477(241.50 - 224.19)$$
$$= 193.56,$$

$$\overline{Y}_{21(adj)} = \overline{Y}_{21} - b_w(\overline{X}_{21} - \overline{X}) = 204.00 - 0.7477(230.00 - 224.19)$$
$$= 199.65,$$

and

$$\overline{Y}_{22(adj)} = \overline{Y}_{22} - b_w(\overline{X}_{22} - \overline{X}) = 186.25 - 0.7477(215.50 - 224.19)$$
$$= 192.75.$$

The graphical presentation (Figure 5) shows clearly that the effects of a package store (factor A) and the licensed restaurant (factor B) are not independent. The fact that the two lines in the graph are not parallel demonstrates this interaction. It can be seen that the effect of establishing a package store seems very minor if no licensed restaurant is established (the B_2 line), while the package store has a significant increasing effect on the accident rate if a licensed restaurant is also established (the B_1 line). These graphical interpretations complement the results of the hypothesis tests on the simple main effects.

In many cases, the researcher may wish to conduct mean comparisons, and where significant interactions exist it would be more helpful if simple main effect mean comparisons were used. However, for the example considered here, each factor has only two levels and the tests of simple main effects have already accomplished all possible simple main effect mean comparisons. In other cases, where significant interactions exist and factors have more than two levels, it may be useful to conduct specific simple main effect mean comparisons in addition to testing the simple main effect hypotheses.

ANALYSIS WITH UNEQUAL CELL SIZES

Even in experimental studies, where the researcher has direct control over the selection and assignment of test units, there are often cases when cell sizes are unequal. There are basically three reasons why an experimental study may have unequal cell sizes. Each of these calls for a different kind of analysis (which will not be discussed in detail here).

The first case is when the researcher chooses, for convenience, to obtain a different number of observations for different levels of the factors, and then assigns the test units to the cells *proportionally*. The reason why the cell sizes differ must be assumed to be independent of the nature of the independent variables. For example, different levels of a categorical variable may require different kinds of interviewers and only a very limited number of each kind is available. The interviews may need to be conducted simultaneously, and the researcher may want to use all available interviewers even though for some factor levels there are more interviewers than for some others. The so-called conventional analysis, an analysis identical to that discussed earlier in this section but with n_i substituted for n in the appropriate places (Kirk, 1968), is appropriate for this kind of situation.

The second case is when the researcher plans to have equal cell sizes, but for reasons unrelated to the nature of the independent variables, data from some test units are not obtained. For example, because of the unavailability of some test units during the study, or because data from some test units must be discarded for various reasons unrelated to the nature of the independent variables. The so-called unweighted means analysis (Kirk, 1968), which is very similar to the analysis discussed in this section is used under these circumstances.

The third case is when the unequal cell sizes are present for reasons related to the nature of independent variables. For example, some respondents may refuse to participate *because of* their membership in a given cell. The analysis technique for this case is the least-squares method. (For a detailed discussion of the least-squares method for unequal cell sizes in factorial design for analysis of variance refer to Winer, 1971.)

Other Designs

From the preceding discussion it should be clear to the reader that covariance analysis may be conducted within the context of any type of design. While it is unrealistic to discuss all possible alternate designs for analysis of covariance, in this section we will briefly consider and provide further references for selected additional experimental designs.

The Latin square design is a somewhat more complex design than those already considered. However, the Latin square may be an effective way to experimentally minimize the effects of two extraneous, or nuisance variables when investigating the impact of alternate levels of a single treatment (categorical independent) variable. This design is somewhat restrictive in the sense that it requires an equal number of levels for each of the two extraneous variables and the treatment variable. The Latin square design results in n^2 cells, where n equals the number of treatment levels. Futhermore, if there are no replications within cells, it is not advisable to conduct a Latin square analysis with fewer than five treatment levels because this provides too few degrees of freedom for the error term. The computations for the Latin square analysis of covariance are relatively similar to those used in conjunction with the randomized complete block design. If the reader is familiar with the computations for the regular Latin square analysis of variance and the basic principles of the analysis of covariance as described in conjunction with the randomized complete block design, it should be fairly easy to understand the computations relating to the analysis of covariance for Latin square designs. For a discussion and numeric examples of the Latin square analysis of covariance the reader is referred to Federer (1955), Snedecor (1956), and Ostle (1963).

The use of blocking has been discussed within the context of the completely randomized design. However, sometimes it is useful to use blocking in conjunction with a factorial design, in which case the design is referred to as a randomized block factorial design. The analysis for this design may be viewed as an extension of analysis of covariance for either the factorial design or the randomized complete block design. This extension is straightforward and involves an increase in the number of variables. For a discussion and numeric examples for the randomized block factorial analysis of covariance the reader is referred to Steel and Torrie (1960) and Ostle (1963).

One might also find applications of analysis of covariance with respect to various repeated designs, such as the split plot design. For a discussion of analysis of covariance in conjunction with repeated designs the reader is referred to Winer (1971). Also, Zelen (1957) discusses the analysis of covariance for incomplete block designs, and Cornish (1940) discusses the analysis of covariance for various quasi-factorial designs.

REFERENCES

BLALOCK, H. M. (1972) Social Statistics. New York: McGraw-Hill.

BLAU, P. M. and O. D. DUNCAN (1967) American Occupational Structure. New York: John Wiley.

CORNISH, E. A. (1940) "The analysis of covariance in quasi-factorial designs." Annals of Eugenics 10: 269-279.

ELASHOFF, J. C. (1969) "Analysis of covariance: a delicate instrument." American Educational Research Journal 6: 383-401.

FEDERER, W. T. (1955) Experimental Design. New York: Macmillan.

FEIERABEND, I. K. and R. L. FEIERABEND (1972) "Coerciveness and change: cross-national trends." American Behavioral Scientist 15: 911-927.

GLASS, G. V., P. D. PECKHAM and J. R. SANDERS (1972) "Consequences of failure to meet assumptions underlying the fixed effects analysis of variance and covariance." Review of Educational Research 43: 237-288.

IVERSON, G. R. and H. NORPOTH (1976) Analysis of Variance. Sage University Paper on Quantitative Applications in the Social Sciences, series no. 07-001. Beverly Hills and London: Sage Publications.

KIRK, R. E. (1968) Experimental Design: Procedure for the Behavioral Sciences. Belmont, CA: Brooks/Cole.

LORD, F. M. (1967) "A paradox in the interpretation of group comparisons." Psychological Bulletin 68: 304-305.

——— (1969) "Statistical adjustments when comparing preexisting groups." Psychological Bulletin 72: 336-337.

OSTLE, B. (1963) Statistics in Research. Ames: Iowa State University Press.

PASTERNACK, B. and G. CHAREN (1969) "A simplified guide to covariance analysis using two concomitant variables illustrated on data from an experiment in education." Science Education 53: 78-88.

PECHMAN, P. D. (1968) "An investigation fo the effects of non-homogeneity of regression slopes upon the F-test of analysis of covariance." Laboratory of Educational Research, Report No. 16. Boulder: University of Colorado.

SNEDECOR, G. W. (1956) Statistical Methods Applied to Experiments in Agriculture and Biology. Ames: Iowa State University Press.

STEEL, R. G. and J. H. TORRIE (1960) Principles and Procedures of Statistics. New York: McGraw-Hill.

STOKOLS, D., T. E. SMITH, and J. J. PROSTOR (1975) "Partitioning and perceived crowding in a public space." American Behavioral Scientist 18: 792-814.

WINER, B. J. (1971) Statistical Principles in Experimental Design. New York: McGraw-Hill.

ZELEN, M. (1975) "The analysis of covariance for incomplete block designs." Biometrics 13: 309-332.

APPENDIX

Model Assumptions and Sensitivity

Statistical models for analysis of covariance in various design contexts have been stated earlier and specific assumptions relevant to those models have been noted when required by the discussion. The intent of this section is to state the model assumptions in explicit form, and to provide a discussion of the consequences of violating the assumptions. (For further reading in this area see Elashoff [1969] and Glass, Peckham and Sanders [1972].) The following discussion will explicitly consider the completely randomized design but, in general, will apply to other contexts.

The algebraic form of the statistical model for analysis of covariance in the context of a completely randomized design is given by equation (1). To use the analysis of covariance technique in a valid manner, the following assumptions are made:

(1) The scores on the dependent variable are a linear combination of four independent components: an overall mean, a treatment effect, a linear covariate effect, and an error term.

(2) The error is normally and independently distributed with mean zero and variance σ_ϵ^2.

(3) The (weighted) sum over all groups of the treatment/group effect is zero.

(4) The coefficient of the covariate (slope of the regression line) is the same for each treatment/group.

(5) The covariate is a fixed mathematical variable measured without error, not a stochastic variable.

The first assumption incorporates four points: additivity, linearity of regression, independence of the error component from the predictive factors included in the model, and independence of the covariate from the treatment effects. As with analyses of variance, the principal effect of employing an additive model when the underlying process is nonadditive is a loss of information. Most authors conclude that violation of this additivity assumption should not be a prime concern for researchers. In certain cases, severe departure from an additive model may be corrected by variable transformations. For example, a multiplicative model may be transformed via log transformation into an additive model. In addition to additivity, the covariance model assumes a linear relationship between the covariate and the dependent variable. If this assumption is seriously violated the mean comparisons may be biased. If the researcher is concerned about the viability of the linearity assumption there are two basic options available. The assumption may be tested statistically or scatter diagrams may be prepared for each group to determine if the relationship between the covariate and the dependent variable departs greatly from linearity. The assumption concerning the independence of the error term from the predictive (i.e., nonrandom) elements of the model is a necessary requisite for conducting the statistical analysis both in analysis of variance and analysis of covariance. Violation of this assumption may lead to serious consequences. However this does not present much of a problem to the researcher in experimental studies, since this independence can be assured by the random assignment of test units to treatment groups. The final part of this assumption, that the covariate is independent of the treatment, is a basic tenet of the analysis of covariance model. When the covariate and treatment are not independent, the regression adjustment may obscure part of the treatment effect or may produce spurious treatment effects. This difficulty can be avoided in experimental contexts by measuring the covariate prior to the administration of the treatments and assigning the treatments to test units at random. It is noted that with nonexperimental studies violation of this assumption may seriously affect the interpretation of results.

The second assumption involves three points: normality, homogeneity of variance, and independence of error. These are the assumptions upon which the F-test is based. (It should be noted that in the analysis of covariance framework, the e_{ij}'s are residuals about the within group regression line estimated via a common slope, and the common variance is the error variance of the estimate.) Most researchers indicate that the analysis of covariance model is robust with respect to violations of the assumptions of normality and homogeneity of variance, as is the analysis of variance model. However, there are some indications that the model sensitivity to these assumptions may be affected by the values of the covariates (see Glass et al., 1972: 274-275). Also, as in analysis of variance, nonindependence of errors can have serious effects on the validity of probability statements relative to the statistical tests. Although no adequate measure of the degree of independence of errors within groups exists, this problem is usually circumvented in experimental studies by the careful design of the experiment to insure that independence is preserved.

The third assumption, the summation of the weighted treatment effects is zero, is more of a restriction placed upon the model than an assumption. By specifying treatment means as the sum of two components, the overall mean and the increment for each treatment, the researcher satisfies this restriction.

The fourth assumption is the homogeneity of regression assumption. It states that the slope of the regression line (i.e., the incremental impact of the covariate) is the same for all treatment groups. In other words, there are no treatment-slope interactions. Little study has been done on the effects of violations of this assumption. The work most relevant to typical research applications (Pechman, 1968) is based on findings obtained from Monte Carlo simulations. Pechman found that the empirical sampling distribution of the F-statistic differed little from the theoretical distribution unless the departures from homogeneous slopes were extreme. His work indicates that, as the situation departs from homogeneous slopes, the analysis becomes more conservative with respect to making a type I error. These results were obtained under conditions which required the distribution of the covariate to be the same for each treatment group. A second phase of his investigation suggests that the robustness continues to hold in quasi-experimental settings in which the distributions of the covariate (or covariate means) differ by treatment group. As the reader is aware, statistical tests exist for examining the heterogeneity of regression slopes.

The analysis of covariance procedure is based on the assumption that the covariate is fixed and measured without error. Violations of this assumption occur when the covariate is either random and/or measured with error. Limited available research indicates that if the covariate is a random variable measured without error there is little effect on the F-test. And, in those situations where error in measurements are involved, the major impact appears to be a lowering of the precision of the analysis. For a more complete discussion of this matter refer to Glass et al. (1972: 279-281).

ALBERT R. WILDT is associate professor of marketing at the University of Georgia, on leave of absence from the University of Florida. He received a Ph.D. in industrial administration from Purdue University in 1972. Dr. Wildt is a member of the editorial boards of the Journal of Marketing and the Journal of Marketing Research. His articles have appeared in several scholarly journals, including the Journal of Marketing Research, Management Science, and the Journal of Consumer Research.

OLLI T. AHTOLA is assistant professor of marketing at the University of Florida. He received his Ph.D. from the University of Illinois in 1973. Dr. Ahtola is a member of the editorial board of the Journal of Marketing. His articles have appeared in such professional publications as Journal of Marketing Research, Journal of Consumer Research, and Journal of Population. His interests include the development of models to predict and understand consumer attitudes, intentions, and purchase behavior.

NOTES